Real Women with Real Praise
for the Lean Out Message

"Thank you to you and your Lean Out message. I've been looking for words to put to my feelings and your message is exactly how I'm feeling! I can't wait to read more and learn to Lean Into my personal life more than my work life."
- Jaime B., mother of one,
property manager

"I just want you to know how much your message spoke to me. I appreciate your message and hope that other women discover it and identify with it, too!"
- Anonymous, mother of two,
occupational therapist

"Great job starting this topic! My eyes have been opened to things I never knew existed for women who are both Leaning In and Leaning Out."
- Megan M., mother of four,
entrepreneur

"I'm so happy to have found you! I just went back to work after my second baby and immediately decided I need to lean out!! I'm so glad I'm not alone in this feeling!!"
- Alicea A., mother of two, former
corporate Lean-Inner

"I've been practicing a lot of Lean Out. I'm choosing my family and my sanity over what society thinks I need to be doing."
- Kristina N., mother of three, blogger

MONICA E. PIERCE

LEANING OUT

AN *ALTERNATIVE* PERSPECTIVE FOR THE
FOR THE
MODERN CORPORATE WOMAN

gatekeeper press
Columbus, Ohio

Leaning Out: An Alternative Perspective for the Modern Corporate Woman

Published by Gatekeeper Press
2167 Stringtown Rd, Suite 109
Columbus, OH 43123-2989
www.GatekeeperPress.com

Cover Design by Books-Design.com

Library of Congress Control Number: 2019953909

ISBN (hardcover): 9781642378641
ISBN (paperback): 9781642378658
eISBN: 9781642378665

For my immortality project -
Everett, Anastasia, and Tommy

Contents

Introduction

Who I Am

I am no one you've ever heard of. I'm not a household name like Sheryl Sandberg or Megyn Kelly or Rachel Hollis. I'm not a notable public figure or a highly accomplished business professional. I'll never appear on Forbes' *Top 30 Under 30* list for achieving great wealth or power. I haven't launched a billion-dollar startup. I haven't had a blog post go viral overnight. I don't speak on panels or at university commencement ceremonies. And although I have a solid education including a master's degree, neither of my alma maters carries any name recognition outside of California.

So why should you care what I have to say? Why did you decide to pick up this book when it was probably sitting next to one with an author much more noteworthy than me? Because the fact that I am average is the very point. Like you, I am an actual modern career woman.

While my résumé might not stand out much, I've survived 15 years in the middle ranks of the modern corporate world while nurturing a loving marriage and raising three rambunctious, beautiful children. I've done the performance evaluations, the design reviews, the team happy hours and the women-in-leadership conferences, all while handling maternity leaves, pumping sessions, daycare drama and vacation time used to stay home with sick kids. I'm your average working woman in corporate America. But I'm not average because I've somehow failed to climb the ranks or make a name for myself. *I'm average because I've deliberately chosen to be.*

Unlike the big-name authors of the books sitting next to mine, I'm not here to urge you to "Lean In" or to give you 10 magical tips for how to "Have it All." There are enough voices in your life already doing just that. I want to offer you another option. I want you to critically consider what "having it all" actually means and instead think about designing a life around having only what you want, especially if what you want does *not* include a corner office.

Who We Are

This alternative message is for professional women who want a fulfilling career but do not want to climb up the corporate leadership ranks solely out of obligation. It's for us women who are confident in our choices yet sometimes feel guilty for not striving to reach our greatest professional potential. This message is for women who want to Lean Out when the world is urging us to Lean In. It's for women who think something must be wrong with us because we lack the baseline ambition every other professional woman around us seems to have.

We're mistakenly identified as either the working mother who's always frazzled, the victimized office female who's oppressed by sexist colleagues, or the corporate go-getter who doesn't have time for marriage or a family because she's busy kicking ass. But we aren't any of these extreme clichés. We are respected, successful and balanced women who have it together. We are fortunate because, for us, there is no "glass ceiling" of low self-esteem, sexist leaders, high childcare costs or unequal pay. We don't feel limited by the fact that we're female. On the contrary. We're fortunate to have so much opportunity and confidence to pursue it that we actually feel obligated to achieve as much as we possibly can. We feel guilty if we're not accomplishing the amazing things we know we're capable of. We are stuck in an uncomfortable, misunderstood space between great professional potential and conflicting personal ambivalence.

Yet no one ever speaks of us because they don't realize we exist. Image 1 describes the groups that women are commonly associated with and where we actually fit in amongst them.

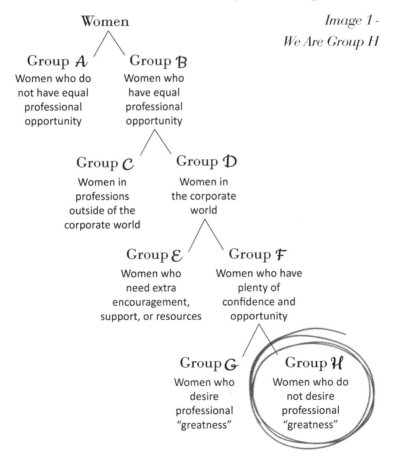

Image 1 - We Are Group H

Group A is where we women have found ourselves since the dawn of time. It's where the women's movement originated and continues to live. As long as there are still women in this category, we must continue fighting for them because we all agree that every single woman deserves the same opportunities as her male peers. Eventually, this group will disappear entirely because all women will have equal opportunity.

Group B is all of us who benefited from the original women's movement and now have the same access to education and professional opportunity as our male peers. Many women's rights advocates feel Group A and B are mutually exclusive. They believe there is no Group B until *all* members of Group A have equal opportunity, which is why they still paint such a broad brush when preaching for women's equality, even though they're often preaching to those of us who already have it.

Group C is women who have equal opportunity and work in areas other than the corporate world (such as education, medicine, or the arts) or they are stay-at-home-parents. It's likely that these women are not familiar with the pressure to Lean In and achieve impressive titles or power because it is something that is fairly unique to those of us in the corporate world. They might have scheduled work hours so they aren't exposed to the corporate politics world where one's value is inferred based on how many hours are put in at the office or how late at night one continues responding to emails. Women in Group C have their own set of challenges and their roles are just as demanding as those of us in the corporate world. But they are a different set of challenges making some of what we'll talk about in this book not as relevant for women in this group.

Group D is all of us who work in the corporate world and are urged daily to climb the ladder and Lean In. Conferences, magazine articles... everywhere we turn, we're hit with stories about "why we need more women at the top," "here are some amazing women who made it to the top" and "how you can get to the top." There is never any mention of anything other than getting to the top. This is where the issue begins.

Group E is women who work in the corporate world, hear the recurring message to "get to the top," but need a little extra encouragement to get there. These are the women who benefit from popular organizations like Lean In Circles and mainstream books and messages like *Girl, Stop Apologizing* from Rachel Hollis and *You Are a Badass* from Jen Sincero. These women unfortunately do encounter a glass ceiling made up of sexism, intimidating male superiors, high childcare costs, low confidence, a husband who pressures them to "step back from work for a while," or other common hurdles that women face in the corporate world. When these women have sincere aspirations to achieve professional greatness, it is important that they find the support and encouragement to do so. For this reason, it is good that resources and campaigns like Lean In exist.

Group F is those of us who work in the corporate world, face the pressure to Lean In and "get to the top" but do not experience the hurdles faced by Group E. We actually have all of the confidence and opportunity we could ever wish for. We are the women who messages like "Lean In" and "Have it All" are encouraging. We are the ones who the other groups hope will "get to the top" and make changes on their behalf.

Group G are the women in the Corporate world who have all the confidence and opportunity necessary to climb the ladder and actually *want* to achieve the greatness that they're cheered towards. They want to Lean Into their jobs. They want to obtain positions of power so they can represent all of us and help those behind find their way up as well. For these women, we are grateful, we are proud, and we support them!

At this point, the general opinion is that we've captured everyone. But there is one more group hidden within Group F, working in the cubicle next door to Group G.

Group H is where I find myself and where you might be, too. We're misunderstood as being members of Group E because we aren't clamoring for the next promotion, so people think we lack confidence. Or, we're misunderstood as being a part of Group G because we are confident and successful, so it's assumed we want to achieve as much as we possibly can. In lieu of our own group, most of us just pretend we're members of Group G since it's the most socially respected path. Some of us are so good at pretending we're members of Group G that we've even convinced ourselves that we are! And as is in my case, many of us started in Group G with true ambitions to achieve but we've migrated over to Group H, as other priorities have entered our lives and, for various reasons, we no longer have a desire to climb the ladder as far as we possibly can.

Whatever the reason we find ourselves not fitting into Group G with the Lean Inners, we deserve our own group - our own identity. And that's what this book - our message - is about. It's not saying we want to go all the way back to Group A before women had equal opportunity. It's not trying to argue those in the other groups are "wrong." Just as we don't want to be told our perspectives and our decisions are "wrong," we aren't saying that theirs are. We just want to be heard. We want our own spot on the chart. We want to be reassured it's okay if we don't fit into one of the categories that the mainstream expects us to. It's okay if we don't want to climb the ladder even though we know we could.

Purpose of This Book

I'm not here to try and convince those who want to Lean In that they should Lean Out. But today's mainstream media is slanted towards messages for women who want to Lean In. For a number of reasons which we'll discuss in this book, women who don't want to Lean In feel alone and guilty. I want to bring an alternative message and start a dialogue for the rest of us.

Throughout the book I will share my personal perspectives on the corporate world, women in leadership, and some of the mainstream messages with which we're all familiar. My alternative perspectives aren't attempts to argue that I am right, and the mainstream opinion is wrong. No one can be right or wrong in an opinion or when it comes to their own personal experience. I simply want to share a different story and express some different opinions than those we're used to hearing.

It's also important to note that my opinions and perspectives are just that. You won't see me presenting loads of scientific evidence or data from in-depth studies I've conducted, partly because I have a full-time job, three young kids and am writing a book "in my spare time" so I have no bandwidth to become a full-fledged researcher. But also, because it's hard to measure the private thoughts and opinions of an entire population of modern women.

While I may not have objective evidence to support my feelings and opinions, I have anecdotal evidence. My perspectives are rooted in observations of hundreds of co-workers, leaders, public figures and the like; women, men, married, single, parents, not parents. My perspectives are the result of countless conversations with co-workers and friends who've confided in me through the years how they *really* feel about their job and their career, what they *really* think about this Lean In message. Such conversations and observations led to this Lean Out message. I decided to start sharing it on social media where it was received and echoed by thousands of strangers in the online community who confirmed the sentiment.

This book is intended to acknowledge and encourage women who find themselves in Group H. Amongst us, we've probably had similar upbringings and professional experiences, and now lead similar lives which results in us holding these comparable perspectives. But just because we all have these similarities, we recognize that many women have had vastly different experiences and hold different perspectives.

If you are someone who falls into a group *other* than Group H – maybe you don't quite have access to the professional opportunities I speak of, you've been limited and challenged simply for being female, or you are leaning into your career out of sheer passion for your work, then I'm glad you're here, too. You might not agree with or understand the perspectives I share, but I hope you will read them anyway because, just as I acknowledge your unique experience while respecting your opinions and choices, I believe you will do the same for me and mine.

As a community of modern professional women, we all have the same goal to be respected and understood. The intention of this book is not to dismiss the different experiences of certain women or argue that the choices other women have made are wrong. I simply want to speak up for those readers who are in Group H, to let them know they are not alone in having their unique experiences and perspectives, and to reassure them that it's okay if they find they don't fit in with the other more commonly recognized groups of women.

The first half of the book shares my ideas for how we've ended up in this situation in the first place and why we all feel so obligated to Lean In. After exploring the reasons for our obligation to achieve, in the second half of the book I'll share suggestions for how we can Lean Out, as individuals and as a whole.

Throughout the book, I'll share personal stories of my own childhood and early career as well as experiences that led me to start Leaning Out. My hope is that you will walk away with a reassurance that you are not alone if you secretly have no desire to climb the corporate ladder, and you find the confidence to live the life you choose to live, not the one you feel obligated to live.

Part 1
Why We Feel So Obligated

Chapter 1 *The Lean In Message*

"I hope that you—yes, you—each and every one of
you have the ambition to run the world, because
this world needs you to run it. Women all around
the world are counting on you."

- Sheryl Sandberg

I sat in the oversized teal pleather chair, awkwardly holding
my Kindle in my left hand while pressing two Medela shields
to my chest with my right arm. It was August 2013 and I had
just returned to work from my second maternity leave. I was
comfortable and relaxed in the private mothers' room, pumping
away for my 4-month-old son, Everett, who attended daycare full-
time along with his two-year-old brother, Tommy. As I pumped,
I read a new book I'd heard about in some 'working mother'
forum. It was called *Lean In: Women, Work and the Will to
Lead.* It was by a woman I'd never heard of but apparently, she
was someone big at Facebook, the young social media startup
located just up the road from my office in Palo Alto, California.

I was 30 years old and working at the same large defense
contractor where I'd started right out of undergrad eight years

earlier. I had a decent job in program management. I had worked my way through the company's leadership development program and was on a promising career path. Additional responsibility, increasingly impressive titles and a growing salary would all be mine if I wanted them. All I had to do was stay on track; keep "paying my dues" and I would achieve that definition of professional success that had been so ingrained in me since childhood.

In addition to a promising corporate career, my husband Michael and I owned a small house in the heart of Silicon Valley - no small feat, even if it was due in part to the recession and house market crash. I had two business degrees including an MBA from a local university. And on top of all that, I was happily married to my best friend and a mom to two healthy, beautiful little boys. I was well on my way to "having it all" by society's definition of personal and professional accomplishment.

Yet the Kindle screen in my hand was telling me that all of this wasn't enough. First, it was telling me that I had a confidence problem. A fair amount of the book was dedicated to studies and anecdotes about how women tend to underestimate ourselves simply because we're women. The author used many tactics and impassioned arguments in an effort to convince me, the reader, that I was as capable and deserving as my male peers. It was a fact I did not need convincing of since I'd been raised in the '90s when girls were constantly told we were just as capable as the boys. But since her message wasn't necessarily a bad one, that might be relevant for other woman if not for me, I let it be and kept reading.

Second, the book provided tangible advice for how I could succeed in my corporate career even though, according to the book I would apparently encounter sexism and injustices at every turn. It explained to me how I could negotiate for a fair salary and enlist my spouse to support me in a way that would give me a chance at professional success. Again, arguments that made sense but didn't apply to me. I had amazing co-workers, leaders who saw me as a professional and paid me more than fairly, plus a husband who was a true teammate; always doing his part for our family and encouraging me to pursue my dreams... whatever I decided they were.

As the Lean In message continued to fall flat for me, I thought perhaps there was something unusual about my life and my situation. It seemed as though I was the only one who didn't struggle with her own self-worth, with commanding respect from others, or with balancing the demands of her personal and professional life. If such a popular book was presenting solutions to issues that were seemingly so pervasive for modern women in the corporate world, I must just be lucky to not be experiencing those issues myself.

Just when I thought the book wasn't meant for me, the author presented her cornerstone call-to-action which was directed squarely at readers like me: privileged young women with education, confidence, support and opportunity. The book urged us to "Lean In," meaning achieve as much as we possibly could in our professional careers. It reminded us that it was our obligation, on behalf of women everywhere, to capitalize on our opportunity and go after that corner office.

It was a completely logical argument and one that my then people-pleasing self could easily get behind. After all, who doesn't want to assert that their gender is just as capable as the other? Who doesn't want to fight to advance the rights of their own party? Who wouldn't want a position of power and to receive great wealth and respect along with it? So even though I couldn't relate to the book's foundational claims about the challenges faced by women in the modern corporate world, I ate up every word of the call-to-action to Lean In. And without thinking more deeply about what I might actually want for my own life, I dutifully continued on my path up the ladder.

I was just returning from maternity leave and was still getting back into my old corporate-go-getter mode. After having been home with my two young sons and being in raise-good-humans mode for about five months, the project schedules and production reviews I came back to somehow felt less important than I had remembered. I was having trouble motivating myself to care about milestones and resourcing levels when I had two tiny humans counting on me coming home at a reasonable hour. So *Lean In's* call to action was exactly the kick in the pants I thought I needed, to remind me of what I thought my purpose was—the same purpose I'd been told I had ever since childhood—to apply the talents and opportunity I was so blessed with and achieve as much professional success as I could.

But after years of trying to live up to this famous female call-to-action, I continue to struggle with it. Here's why.

Flaw #1 – The Idea That More Women at the Top Will Change Things for the Rest of Us

The charter of Lean In and the modern feminist movement it evolved into goes something like this: the more women we "get into leadership," the more those women can change the professional landscape to the benefit of the rest of womankind. So, the logic continues, if you are fortunate like me, given education, support, opportunity and a chance to "get a seat at the table," you'd better get that seat.

The *Lean In* book itself (including "the Will to Lead" in its subtitle) is a direct attempt to convince us that this level of great professional accomplishment should be our goal in life. If it isn't inherently, we should make it so.

But let's look at an example of one such woman who did exactly what the Lean In message called for. Marissa Mayer, former CEO of Yahoo!, famously took just a few weeks of maternity leave after the birth of her first baby in 2012, and the birth of twins in 2015. Consider what kind of message it would have sent to millions of working mothers if Mayer had taken six, or even just three months of leave! Think about what kind of trail that would have blazed for women who want to be devoted mothers but also pursue high-powered professional positions. But instead, Mayer perpetuated the expectation that women who want to achieve this level of professional success must do so by foregoing personal priorities – that it has to be a trade-off. Of course, we can't know the ins-and-outs of Ms. Mayer's personal life, and the decision of when to return to work from maternity leave is a very complicated and personal one. And yes, many women *want* to return to work as soon as they're able because of the passion they have for their work. In that case, it's great that they have the support and resources to enable them to return to work as soon as they are ready.

Regardless, the argument that getting more women into positions of leadership will change the status quo is proven

> The argument that getting more women into positions of leadership will change the status quo is proven flawed by examples like Mayer.

flawed by examples like Mayer. She reached the top and had an opportunity to do something different from what is expected of high-powered professionals, but instead she perpetuated the unreasonable standard to put your work before all else.

There has been a lot of talk lately around the need for comprehensive maternity and parental leave in the US. While government support for new mothers and parents should be a given, and I agree we should continue pushing for this legislation, just because such laws would make maternity leave available, doesn't mean women will take their full maternity leave. In fact, I wager they wouldn't. It's one thing if a woman *wants* to go back to work sooner than the end of her maternity leave. But it's another if she feels obligated to return sooner than she'd prefer because she believes that if she doesn't go back quickly, then she'll fall behind. Sure, there are women in the former category, but I believe women who go back sooner than the end of their maternity leaves usually do so out of fear of falling behind. Legislating for additional maternity leave won't change women's behavior unless women in leadership positions take full advantage of that benefit, demonstrating that it's acceptable to put other priorities before our careers and still be valuable professionals.

It also seems contradictory to a position that is rooted in equality for these modern feminists to look only to *women* to reach positions of influence and change the standards. Why can't men in leadership roles also help change the culture to enable more working parents to succeed?

Some of the greatest leaders I know are men who are involved, devoted husbands and fathers. In fact, one specific former co-worker comes to mind. At the time I worked with him, he was a well-respected vice president at the software startup we worked at. He decided to leave the job and take a whole year off work, just to be with his kids while they were still young. While this decision probably seemed insane to his peers - high-powered male executives in Silicon Valley - I found it to be one of the most admirable, refreshing decisions I ever saw someone make. That is the kind of leadership we need, and this is how someone can effect change for the rest of us.

Gut Check: If you're a woman "at the top" or in any position of influence, are you setting an example for making the corporate world more manageable, more humane for working parents?

Flaw #2 – The Incorrect Assumption that All Women Want to Achieve as Much as Possible

Recently, my three-year-old daughter and I have been reading this sweet children's book that recognizes amazing women in history. It ends with a call-to-action for the young reader to think about how she herself "will change the world." The very last page has cartoon pictures of Joan of Arc, Lucille Ball, Hillary Clinton, and an open space named "You." Across the top it reads, "How Will You Change the World?"

It's a message that is pervasive in our culture and is viewed as a must for our young girls. But it doesn't bother asking, "Do you *want* to change the world?" It just automatically assumes and expects that we all have this goal. And oh, by the way, the only way you can change the world is through some sort of professional greatness and fame, like the women in the book. Being a good person, raising moral, responsible children, caring for others, and having a rewarding but unremarkable career isn't enough.

I'm not saying we shouldn't encourage our girls to achieve professionally. Of course, we want them to know they *can* do great things if they *want* to. But they don't *have* to be the greatest female comedian or the (almost) first woman President of the United States to be great. Let's change it from "should" do great things back to "can" do great things, keeping in mind that "great things" can be accomplished in mediocre lives, too.

When I read this book with my daughter, in addition to talking about all these amazing women and their noteworthy accomplishments, we also talked about her finding professional fulfillment, helping people, doing something she's passionate about, or being a wife and maybe a mom... that all these things are good too. And Mama will love her, no matter what.

In addition to the automatic assumption that all modern professional women are striving for high-level accomplishment, my daughter's book demonstrates another reason why we bend over backwards to climb the ladder even if we don't want to: it's because we want to serve as an example - as role models - for our daughters. This is an admirable reason, for sure. But for me, once I had a daughter, I realized I didn't want her to see me getting home late from the office, frazzled from my work day, grouchy and stressed over a lack of sleep and pressure from my job, missing her first soccer game because of a work meeting that ran late, or stepping away from a family vacation to join an "important" conference call in the hotel room. Even if my intentions were good, I didn't want to risk my daughter (or my sons) misconstruing my Leaning In as me actually putting my career before them. And I didn't want them to misunderstand my "hustling" as their mom's definition of what "success" in life had to look like.

Even if I were able to avoid such a misinterpretation, the last thing I wanted was for my own daughter to feel pressured to achieve professional success in the way I had felt pressured by society. I would much rather her see me as a balanced, fulfilled woman who is confident in her own decisions. I want her to know that she is "successful" even if she ends up with just an average, decent job that she loves, and, if she chooses, a family of her own. Like all parents, I just want my children to be happy. Of course, if my daughter truly *wants* to climb the ladder and pursue professional greatness, I will support her. But if she has no such ambition, I will support her. It's this latter option that I believe we are failing to show our daughters, and if we don't start expanding the message of what success looks like, we will perpetuate this obligatory Lean In culture for a whole new generation.

Because I have always struggled to find motivation to climb the corporate ladder, feeling pressured to Lean In and "have it all" even though I didn't really want to, I always thought that *I* was the problem - that something was wrong with *me* for not having the professional ambition that all other women around me seemed to have. But then, in a chance encounter with 19th century philosophy, I realized it wasn't just me. It was my human nature.

In his book *The Denial of Death*, Pulitzer Prize winner Ernest Becker explores the concept of immortality projects, or the causa sui, meaning "cause of itself" in Latin. Becker's idea of immortality projects was that, as humans, we are all naturally afraid of dying, but that it's not just the physical death of our bodies that scares us. It's also the fear of being forgotten and of all memory of who we were disappearing entirely from this world. Since science hasn't been able to figure out a way to solve the whole physical death "thing," we have basically accepted our physical death as inevitable, and we instead focus on doing the best we can to fight off that second death, by doing everything in our power to never be forgotten - to build our legacy. In theory, if you can ensure you will always be remembered, then you can be immortal.

So, the concept of immortality projects begs the question: what are you going to do with your relatively short physical life to ensure you are remembered for as long as possible after your body is gone?

If you boil our daily lives down to the simplest facets of why we do anything, we find that an immortality project is at the root of it all: monuments, governments, national parks named in honor of someone, scientific breakthroughs, changing the lives of others, even just making ends meet in order to feed your family so you can, in turn, raise children to carry on your legacy. The reason why any of us do anything is a desire to make a difference in the world and, in turn, be remembered. If you think of someone like Obama or Einstein or Shakespeare or Julius Caesar or even Jesus Christ; some people are going to "live on" for a long time! The more impact you make, the longer you "live."

So, the way in which we choose to spend our precious, limited days is a direct reflection of what we feel is our greatest chance at immortality. What can you pursue that will have the greatest impact and leave the strongest legacy when you leave this world? Whatever the answer is becomes your immortality project!

For some, their focus is on reaching a certain level of professional accomplishment, impacting people with products and services as well as their leadership. For others, it's becoming a famous rock star, writing and performing music that will be remembered for decades. For some, it's trying to go down in history as the first female American president. For others, it's introducing a new technology to the world. For some, it's writing a book and changing the lives of millions (here's hoping). And for many, it's simply raising a child to be a decent human being, with hopes that your genetics, morals, ideals and your memory will be passed on for generations to come. All of these immortality projects have a (hopefully positive) net effect on our world and all are respectable investments of our time and energy.

When I read this description in Becker's work, it was as if he was speaking directly to me. My struggle to find fulfillment in the corporate world wasn't because something was wrong with me, but because my immortality project is raising my children, not my career. I've never been able to Lean Into my career because I don't need—I can't have—*another* immortality project. Especially not one that so often challenges or conflicts with the first one.

> My struggle to find fulfillment in the corporate world wasn't because something was wrong with me, but because my immortality project is raising my children, not my career.

Even for those who aren't parents, you can make your immortality project any number of things. You may have a day job in corporate America but might also be an avid painter. You may decide to make your painting your immortality project and decide to invest the bulk of your time and energy into your painting rather than going "above and beyond" at work in order to climb the corporate ladder.

Becker also describes the natural conflict that arises from humans having different immortality projects. When our immortality project conflicts with another's, we feel it as an attack on our own personal choices...as if that person thinks we chose the wrong thing as our immortality project. We are *dedicating our life* to the wrong thing. That's a pretty powerful feeling to have. Therefore, we are inclined to prove to others that our immortality project is better than a different one that someone else chose. Becker suggests that immortality projects are at the root of every human conflict—from religious wars to family feuds.

Consider the individual I like to call "The One-Upper." I'm sure you've met him or her before, because there's at least one in every office across America. He's the guy at the water cooler "complaining" about how late he stayed at the office the night before. "Aw man, I was here 'til 11pm last night finishing that report!"

The typical response is to be impressed, automatically implying this person's brilliance or commitment just because he stayed so late at the office. Me? I'm not impressed. I actually see someone who is insecure about the fact that they've chosen their career as their immortality project, that they're trying really hard to convince others (and really, themselves) about how worthwhile it is. It's not the choice that bothers me. It's the One-Upper's insecurity with his choice and the need he feels to have that choice validated by the rest of us. It's fine by me if The One-Upper wants to work late hours in the office or on his laptop at home each night. But I'm not going to let it make me doubt my own choices.

As I described in the Introduction, this is precisely why I wrote this book. I want women like me to know that, even if you have a promising corporate career, it's okay if your immortality project is your role as a mom, or some other personal passion. But we also aren't trying to argue our choice is "right" and those who've chosen their career as their immortality project are "wrong." We just want to point out the fact that both are options and that both should be valid choices in the eyes of society.

This idea of conflicting immortality projects also explains the mom shaming that happens between women who have chosen to work full time and women who've chosen to stay at home full time. While each has made their respective choice for their own reasons, we often feel threatened when confronted with a woman who's made the opposite choice that we have. As a result, we often feel compelled to make our case for the immortality project we've chosen.

It is further complicated for women like me who work full time, yet raising our children is our immortality project. We're burdened with "mom guilt" for not being able to dedicate ourselves as much as we'd like to our immortality project. We would much rather be home making dinner for our family than staying late at the office. We're inclined to choose our kid's soccer game over a last-minute deadline that really can wait until tomorrow.

To make it worse, we usually have to keep our true immortality project a secret because society looks down on women who are educated and have professional opportunity but don't make their career their immortality project. So, when we make a choice to put our family first, we feel guilt and shame for not making our career our immortality project.

Regardless of what you choose as your immortality project, it's important to recognize that every individual makes their own choice, and that they've made the choice for their own reasons. The significant flaw of the Lean In message is that it incorrectly assumes everyone in the corporate world has chosen their career as their immortality project. It's perfectly fine if Sheryl Sandberg and others make their careers their immortality project, but it's incorrect of them to assume that's the choice we've all made.

> The significant flaw of the Lean In message is that it incorrectly assumes everyone in the corporate world has chosen their career as their immortality project.

This is why I believe the Lean In message has fallen flat for so many of us. Telling us to Lean Into our careers is like telling us to change our immortality project.

Gut Check: What is your immortality project? Has it changed over time? Have you been holding on to one that no longer fits? Are you honest with yourself and with others about your true immortality project?

Flaw #3 – The One-Sidedness and Extremity of the Message

Those of us who find ourselves in Group H were told incessantly as young girls that we could *be anything we want to be!* We were fortunate to never feel limited simply because we were female. It became trendy to encourage young women, at every turn, to achieve their greatest professional potential. From Take-Your-Daughter-to-Work Day to Agent Scully to The Spice Girls; everywhere we turned we were confronted with cries of "Girl Power!" and constantly reminded we could do anything and be everything. But after years of hearing this one-sided message over and over again, that "could" became a "should." While the human race would always depend on our continued role in childbearing, our having ambition to be a good wife and mother, even while holding down a full-time job, was no longer enough...not if you were an educated woman in the 1990s.

There are a number of factors that have led to this immense obligation those of us in Group H feel to achieve professional "greatness." I believe the greatest reason is that we want so badly to honor those who fought for us to get where we are today. Also, we recognize how fortunate we are, since many women still do not have the opportunities we enjoy. We feel we owe it to them to do as much as we can with the blessings we have. Or maybe the message "you can be anything you want to be!" was imparted a little too well by our Baby Boomer parents and once we internalized the idea, none of us wanted to end up "just average."

Additionally, our over-exposure to social media has us constantly trying to measure up to the greatness that we all publicly project via our LinkedIn profiles and filtered status updates. Finally, the most unsettling reason why the modern women's movement possibly became so extreme is that we're afraid if we don't continue to prove ourselves, "the men" will send us back to the kitchen, barefoot and pregnant.

But we don't have to keep proving ourselves. We don't need to land on Forbes' *Top 30 Under 30* in order to obtain validation. We don't need to post our latest promotion all over social media in order to convince each other how great we are. And yes, we can "be anything we want to be," but that includes the option to just be average.

For those of us in Group H, this fight for equality has gone on too long and too hard. The pendulum has swung too far in the opposite direction. For the millions of us who were fortunate to be born in a time and place where we have the same opportunities as our male peers and we've never felt limited by our gender, these pervasive messages, constantly urging us to Lean In professionally, have become tiresome and even alienating.

Take for example the speech given by Hollywood actress Glenn Close in January 2019 when she accepted the Golden Globe for best actress. It was a wildly popular speech by all accounts, celebrated in the mainstream media as a moment of victory for women. In her speech she honored her late mother, Bettine Moore Close, and her comments went viral. At first glance, it was a harmless speech that anyone would find inoffensive - even inspirational. But to someone like me with a different perspective, it's speeches like Close's that perpetuate the obligation to achieve and cause many women like me to secretly suffer.

Through her tears, Close said, "I'm thinking of my mom, who really sublimated herself to my father her whole life. And in her 80s she said to me, 'I feel I haven't accomplished anything.' And it was so not right." At that point, I thought Close was going to say something like, "Mom didn't realize she'd actually made the greatest accomplishments any person could hope to make in a lifetime. She raised five happy, balanced children, had a fulfilling marriage and died at the age of 90, surrounded by her loved ones. She left a legacy of warmth and affected hundreds of us with her spirit."

But instead, what Close said next was: "...women, we're nurturers. That's what's expected of us. We have our children and we have our husbands, if we're lucky enough, and our partners, whoever. But we have to find personal fulfillment. We have to fill our – you know, follow our dreams. We have to say, 'I can do that, and I should be allowed to do that.'"

Yes, we should all be allowed to follow our dreams. No one is arguing that. In fact, for those of us in Group B and beyond (most of us who grew up in the '90s or later), we already know we "can do that" and we feel "allowed to do that." Close's message almost feels like it came straight out of the '70s. I don't disagree with her that we should all be "allowed to do that," but for all of us in Groups B and beyond, we know we can. We don't need reminding. Constantly banging on this "we can do it!" drum has an adverse impact on the women who know they "can do it" by making us feel *obligated* to "do it."

Close was pointing out that her mother wasn't enabled to pursue professional goals as she may have wanted to, and that truly is a disappointment because we all should be allowed to do as much (or as little) as we want professionally. But Close also inadvertently implied that professional accomplishment is the best way to measure the value of one's life.

The problem is, Close used her mother's own disappointment as a way of demonstrating that women should feel compelled to do more than "just be mothers." And yes, since having been told from the dawn of time that women can only be mothers, it is important to remind ourselves that that is no longer the case.

In my opinion, the pendulum has swung too far. Now *all* we hear are speeches like Close's urging women to do more than "just be mothers." The point is, we should be hearing *both* messages – women can Lean Into a professional dream if they want, but their life is not wasted if they choose not to.

Close's speech addresses the former, but the latter was missed and is rarely mentioned in today's culture as a viable option for women who are blessed with education and opportunity.

As a mother herself, I doubt Close intended her comment to mean that motherhood is invaluable. But intentional or not, that's how it might have come across to mothers who've sacrificed a professional career to devote themselves to raising their children. Rather than using her mother as an example of how impactful it can be to raise five children (including a famous Hollywood actress), Close used her mother's story as an example of disappointment and shortcoming of one's potential.

A woman who truly desires to pursue professional greatness should be allowed to do so. The problem is that this is the *only* choice that is propped up as admirable in today's society. For women who are mothers and have professional careers, pervasive messages like Close's tell us that motherhood pales in comparison to professional achievement. Apparently, society will value us for our impressive résumé, not for bringing decent human beings into the world. So modern working mothers feel pressured to put work commitments before their families, out of fear of being viewed as not meeting their full potential.

> Pervasive messages like Close's tell us that motherhood pales in comparison to professional achievement.

Due to this one-sidedness of the Lean In message, women who choose *not* to achieve their greatest professional potential are stigmatized.

Recently, a stranger tracked down my LinkedIn profile then used my experience to shame me on one of my social media accounts. She said, "You have an MBA and tenure at Lockheed Martin. You have no explanation for not achieving more. Try harder." I chalked her aggression up to the insanity that is Social Media. But the point is this is precisely the mentality of our society when it comes to what is expected of women like us. If you've been blessed with opportunity yet you don't seize every last morsel of it at all costs; if you don't beat the drum of "Lean In!" and "Girl Power!" then you must be a narrow-minded and lazy anti-feminist. This is the exact mentality that we need to start confronting and changing.

I'm not arguing that we should go back to how things were in the '40s and '50s, when women like Close's mother didn't have equal opportunity. We should all have the *opportunity* to achieve as much as we want. And, if you're someone who decides for yourself that you honestly want to achieve great professional success, then you should be able to! And for Glenn Close who did just that, we celebrate her. But that path shouldn't be the only admirable option. This is the fundamental flaw with the Lean In message and what's become the modern women's movement, as demonstrated by the way Close's speech was seen as so innocuous. If you are a woman in the corporate world, all you ever hear is "Follow your dreams!" and "You can do it!" and "Lean In!" The message is never followed up with, "and it's okay if your dream is just a decent job in middle management with a reasonable schedule which allows you to be home every night with your family." Or, if you simply want to be a full-time stay at home parent. No, that would be a disappointment.

Close's acceptance speech is just one example. But if you start to look, you'll notice that most of the messages we are exposed to are about how we can achieve more, do more, *be* more, implying that who we are naturally when we are being our authentic selves is not enough; that we should be constantly striving to "improve" even if who we are is perfectly fine.

Think about who we recognize in our society and for what reasons we recognize them. There's no Forbes list of "Top 30 Most Balanced People in the World." It's always the "Most Powerful," "Most Influential" or "Richest." Even within channels that are intended to support and lift up working mothers like us, the feature piece of *Working Mom* magazine usually highlights the woman who "has it all." She's CEO of her own company, *and* she has 2.5 beautiful children *and* a fit, stylish look. How does she do it? Then the piece proceeds to tell us how we, too, can be like her.

But for every woman who is CEO and "having it all," there are millions of us who are just mediocre. Yet because we're not meeting the apparent standard of "success," because we don't see average women like us gracing the cover of magazines, we often feel like we're failing even though, actually, we're doing just fine. It's even possible that we are happier and more balanced than CEO Chick who is overworked and perpetually stressed out. Of course, we can't know for sure. She very well could love her job and find a way to make time for her family, hobbies, exercise, etc. But the point is, these are the *only* "success stories" we see: the mythical woman who has made it to the top and "has it all."

I'm not saying we shouldn't celebrate those who accomplish great things, especially if it's something that they truly wanted and fought hard to get. The problem is that "greatness" is the *only* thing we ever seem to celebrate or recognize.

Personally, I'd much rather read a feature piece about Sarah from the suburbs. Sarah has a master's degree in engineering. She has a successful career at a local engineering firm and was recently offered a coveted leadership position at her company. While a voice in her head instinctively told Sarah that she has to take the position because she should Lean In and "women all around the world are counting on her," Sarah turns down the position because it would have placed too much strain on her health and her family. She instead chooses a moderate but respectable career that allows her to raise a happy, healthy family and gives her the opportunity to put her personal happiness first. Sarah takes her kids to soccer practice at 5 p.m. twice a week. She exercises in the evenings once the kids are asleep and then chats for a while in her pajamas on the couch with her husband before they turn in at a reasonable hour.

Sarah is the woman I want to read about. Sarah also deserves respect and recognition, just as CEO Chick does.

Gut Check: What do you aspire to? What are the reasons you aspire to those things? Is it internally driven or is it because they are the things society and others tell you that you should aspire to?

Lack of confidence, sexual harassment, unequal pay, high childcare costs, these are the reasons often used to explain why more women aren't "climbing the ladder." While these are real issues for some women (in which case we have to continue fighting to eradicate them), for those of us in Group H, the reason we aren't climbing the ladder is because we just don't want to. Our immortality project is simply something other than our career. But this doesn't make us bad employees or anti-feminists. We've simply made a different life choice. And just as those who choose to Lean In deserve to be supported, so do we.

Chapter 2 *Our Obsession with Greatness*

"We need far less excellence than we cultivate."
- *Daniel S. Milo*

America is obsessed with greatness: from Tom Brokaw's New York Times Bestseller, *The Greatest Generation* to Donald Trump's infamous 2016 presidential campaign slogan, "Make America Great Again." Even when searching online for books about mediocrity or being average, every single result that comes up is about how to *overcome* average or *defeat* mediocrity. It's an ironic fixation, considering America is arguably substandard in so many ways (education, healthcare, gun violence, physical health, etc.). Yet we have this inflated sense of self - this grandiosity - that trickles down to the lives we lead as individuals and the pedestal upon which we place this thing called "greatness." Plus, for we Xennials and Millennials who were raised to think we're each destined for "greatness," we're experiencing an unintended consequence of that message as we settle into mid-adulthood and find that anything we achieve short of "greatness" feels like a failure.

Survival of the "Good Enough"

In the animal kingdom, the fittest of the species who are best adapted for their environment will survive and thrive. As humans, and especially humans in the corporate world, the measures of such "fitness" are money, titles, and power. She with the most of these will survive. But according to French-Israeli philosopher Daniel S. Milo, author of *Good Enough: The Tolerance for Mediocrity in Nature and Society,* we don't have to be the "greatest" or have the most money or power in order to survive. We just have to be good enough.

In the animal kingdom, not only does the strongest lioness in all of Africa survive, but a moderately strong lioness is also able to kill a gazelle and feed her cubs. In the corporate world, not only are VPs able to feed their families, but a mid-level manager is also able to provide.

Along this line of thinking, Milo also describes the concept of waste and excess as a way of arguing that the "good enough" may actually be better off than the "fittest" or greatest. In the context of the animal world, such waste could be the expenditure of physical energy that doesn't gain the creature any additional benefit. For humans in the modern corporate world, it might be working an extra 10 hours a week for no real gain in productivity or money or taking a promotion that you don't actually want and won't provide you with any additional benefit.

Milo goes on to summarize the biological reason *why* our modern society is wrought with such waste. He explains, "This excess is unavoidable because we have little to do from a survival standpoint. Humans have the ultimate luxury of wasting time and resources in order to divert ourselves. The skills our ancestors cultivated for the purpose of survival no longer serve that purpose. Yet the skills remain. We have the means to achieve ends we no longer need to worry about. So, the means become ends in themselves. Our excess bubbles and blooms not because it is selected through a process of struggle, but because there is no struggle: competition within society is a fool's game. We need far less excellence than we cultivate. We do it anyway because the best of our neurons - those that rescued us from extinction - are underemployed and overqualified. Not because doing so is necessary or even in many cases...useful. More often, it is crushing."

If we apply what Milo says to our modern world—specifically, the corporate world—humans are channeling our natural inclinations to "fight for survival" into a made-up world of business, politics, recreation... simply because we have nothing else to do with ourselves.

Generally speaking, as humans we have all we need: access to food, water, shelter, healthcare, security, and much, much more. We don't each have to raise cattle and grow every single crop we might ever want to consume. We've outsourced that to farmers and grocery stores. We don't each individually have to be on constant alert to defend our own lives and the lives of our offspring. We have police and national defense to do that. As humans, we've developed such elaborate systems of specification and outsourcing that we're left with a vast amount of extra time and mental energy on our hands. But as Milo explains, our inclinations to hunt, fight and provide are

> Humans are channeling our natural inclinations to "fight for survival" into a made-up world of business, politics, recreation... simply because we have nothing else to do with ourselves.

still very much present in our human DNA. So, we've created outlets through which we can apply these urges. We busy ourselves with tasks and seemingly important pursuits, even if they aren't necessary. Could it be? A scientific argument for Leaning Out?

Someone Leaning Into her career beyond a level that brings her resources (money) and satisfaction (professional fulfillment) that she actually wants or needs, is simply excess energy that doesn't need to be spent.

Of course, for someone who is climbing the career ladder because they need the bigger salary or out of pure enjoyment for the work and the additional challenge, doing so is not "waste." Waste comes into the equation when those of us who have all that we want and need still pursue more—more money, more recognition, more power—simply because the option is there.

Gut Check: What pursuits or activities do you have in your life that don't bring you any value, but you do anyway because you feel obligated?

So, How Much is "Enough?"
In 2018, researchers at Purdue University published a study titled "Happiness, income satiation and turning points around the world," in *Nature: International Journal of Science.*

This study analyzed data from over 1.7 million people in 164 countries and found that the global average annual income for one individual to live a comfortable life (eat, pay their bills, buy the basics, etc.) was $60,000–$75,000. In the United States and Canada, it's $105,000. Of course, the number is higher in certain locations and for households that have higher expenses (like multiple kids). Incremental increases after this point actually diminish the individual's happiness.

The study was widely covered in the media and caught my attention at the time, first of all because the ideal amount was interestingly right at my own level of income but also because it was more scientific evidence that Leaning In will not actually make you happier. Of course, there is great ambiguity around how this study or any of us even define the state of "happiness." But the point is, the global directive of the modern women's movement that pressures all women to "climb the ladder" seems to overlook this fact that professional accomplishment in the form of titles, money or power does not necessarily equate to more happiness. Now, if the Lean In movement is asking us to "take one for the team" and Lean In purely to empower the rest of women who do not yet have equal opportunity, that is a different argument and one that I challenged in chapter one. The simplistic case for Leaning In comes with the assumption that you, as an individual, will find fulfillment and happiness by doing so. This study proves what most of us already inherently know; that this is not actually the case.

The Purdue study doesn't attempt to explain *why* people with more money are unhappy, but those of us who work in the corporate world could make some educated guesses. Higher pay usually brings people management and other additional responsibilities, which in turn come with added stress, longer hours, and an expectation to be available when needed, even during family time. Sure, more money can buy us more things, but our ability to sit back and *enjoy* those things decreases. The corporate salary ladder has diminishing returns and, apparently after the $100,000 mark, the more you earn, the less value you actually get from that incremental income. The personal price of earning those extra dollars is not worth it.

So, if you've reached this peak point of income, you don't get additional intrinsic fulfillment from increased responsibility, and you are not motivated by external approval in the form of titles or power, then there is really no reason to Lean In any further. If it's scientifically arguable that it's better to just be mediocre than exceptional, why then, don't we see more media celebrating the victories of everyday life? Why do we continue to hold up the "greatest" and measure ourselves against these unattainable – and what may be undesirable – standards? Because we were raised to value and pursue greatness. We've been told our whole lives - for the entirety of modern human existence - that the greater you are the better, and the more likely you are to survive. Even for those of us who consider ourselves members of Group H, we still probably have an adverse reaction when we hear the word "mediocre." I even had an editor urge me to use a different word, assuming I couldn't have meant to use that word. No, the point is it should be okay to be mediocre. We should be perfectly content living average, "good enough" lives.

> It should be okay to be mediocre. We should be perfectly content living average, "good enough" lives.

But it's in our DNA to achieve, to never be satisfied, to want to be better than our neighbor. We instinctively think that only the giraffe with the longest neck will survive. Only the caveman who brings home the best kill will procreate and pass on his genes. We've been led to believe that only the fittest survive. Mediocrity is not an option.

Gut Check: What amount of money or level of professional challenge is "enough" for you? For your family? Once you've determined this, have you aligned your current job and priorities to ensure you aren't "going over" what you actually want – and making waste for yourself?

My Own Pursuit of "Greatness"

One of my fondest childhood memories is from early 1990, when I was seven years old and spent hours working with my dad on a small model of the house he was planning to build when we moved from California to Arizona. The previous Fall, the San Francisco Bay Area had been rocked by a major earthquake, and it rattled my dad so much that he was ready to leave his dream home in California and move his family to Arizona, where the worst natural disaster is a "dry heat."

Fortunately, his nerves eventually settled, and we didn't go anywhere. But the hours I spent creating and imagining with him over that model stuck with me. I so enjoyed the creative process that my parents and close family friends started telling me I should be an architect when I grew up. I was excited to learn there was a name for this designing of houses and spaces, and that as a grown-up I could do that as my *job*.

Throughout my childhood, my mom would take me to random open houses, just to let my imagination run wild and explore the spaces of strangers. While most kids my age loved going to the park or the skating rink, my favorite thing to do on a Saturday morning was go to the local RV dealership where they let me climb around and explore the open models.

I even had my own game of playing "architect." The hall closet in the middle of our home became the elevator up to my corner office (which doubled as my bedroom when playtime was over). I had a briefcase full of drawings of houses and RVs, and even had a business name.

As a high school senior, when the time came to pick a college and a major, the decision was easy. With a childhood dream of becoming an architect, it had been suggested that I go to California Polytechnic State University, in the beautiful town of San Luis Obispo (a.k.a. Cal Poly SLO) which had a very reputable Architecture school.

So, in the fall of 2001, I found myself at Cal Poly SLO, majoring in Architectural Engineering. In addition to some general ed classes, my initial course load included a class in Engineering Calculus. To say that I struggled would be an understatement. While school had never been especially easy for me, it had never been *impossible* either. But my ability to grasp those engineering concepts was just that: impossible. I sought help, but all the tutors and office hours in the world couldn't save me. It just didn't click, and I failed the class. With many more years of engineering courses in front of me, I knew I wouldn't survive. Fortunately, there was a nice back-up option for kids like me who were hard working, good with people, and not "engineering" smart but "street" smart. So, just two quarters into my college career, I changed my major to Business Administration.

The next quarter I took Business Calculus (the watered-down version of the class I failed) and I aced it. From that point on it was clear I was going to be a businesswoman (whatever that meant). After abandoning my passion for architecture before ever really trying to pursue it, I settled for a field that I was naturally good at.

I had chosen a path that was more likely to result in professional success rather than the path where my heart truly wanted to go, all because I was fixated on achieving "greatness."

My final year of college, I was recruited by Lockheed Martin: a major corporation that was recruiting for their early career leadership development program. I vaguely knew of the company from a childhood neighbor who had worked there his whole career (like most Lockheed employees do). I knew they were a defense contractor which meant they built highly technical products for the military, like stealth planes and protected satellites.

But really, I didn't know much about their products or the defense industry. Unlike my Aerospace and Mechanical Engineering co-workers I would come to meet who had dreamed of a career with this prestigious company, a job there had never crossed my mind (especially back when I thought I was going to be an architect, since Lockheed doesn't design many houses).

However, I knew they were a solid employer: a 100-year-old company that employs over 100,000 people globally. I knew they'd give me decent pay, good benefits, and solid work experience - all things that would allow me to "check the box." They flew me across the country for my interview, put me up in (what to me was) a fancy hotel, toured me and the other candidates around their impressive corporate headquarters, and pitched us their seemingly elite "leadership development program." Subconsciously, I was convinced I could accumulate

a lot of external approval with a career there and work towards
a job title that would allow me to say I had achieved professional
"greatness."

Part of the interview process included a parade of
corporate so-and-so's telling us that we'd all been hand selected
for our academic success and our leadership potential. During
our breaks between these programs, the other candidates
didn't seem too keen on talking to each other. Most of them
were from the East Coast, private colleges, and were much
more experienced in this cutthroat business world. But being
the friendly California girl I was, I managed to chit chat with
a few of them.

Each person I met, dressed in clean business attire,
convinced me either directly or indirectly that if I followed their
lead, I would receive all the professional external approval
I could ever ask for, in the form of a competitive salary and
fancy sounding titles. Sure, I might not know what the hell
I was doing, but if I was good at it, that wouldn't matter.

I came back from that interview process badly wanting
to be selected for the coveted openings in the elite "leadership
development program." In hindsight, it wasn't because I was
passionate about the work I would be hired to do, but because
I wanted the external approval of these strangers. I wanted to
hear that I had been evaluated and determined to be better
than (or at least as good as) the other candidates.

Sure enough, I received an offer and I proudly took the job.
Over the following years, I would get very good at pretending
I was passionate about my chosen path of "businesswoman."
I never again thought about a career in architecture, even
though to this day I'm still moved by a building with a grand
entryway or a cleverly-designed floorplan.

Gut Check: What things have you pursued in your life out of a desire to be "successful" over following your heart?

The Definition of a "Strength"

During my first years in the leadership development program at Lockheed Martin, we were all sent to a workshop that was designed around the Myers-Briggs Type Indicator (MBTI). Derived from the work of Swiss psychologist Carl Jung, mother-and-daughter team Katharine Cook Briggs and Isabel Briggs Myers created an introspective questionnaire based around four principal psychological functions - sensing, intuiting, feeling, and thinking. Its original form, first published in 1944, asks a series of questions to determine where your personality falls within these four parameters.

At the age of 23, as a young professional still learning who I was, the questionnaire told me that I was an ENFJ. The result was fairly consistent with who I believed I was. The "E" stood for Extroversion and, as good as I am at speaking in front of groups and making small talk with strangers, I don't really *like* doing those things. I would much rather spend a day alone in my cubicle, working diligently on a project, than out interacting with other humans.

But at that stage in my life I was still beholden to what others expected of me, what others wanted from me, the type of person others had always told me I should be. In order to Lean In and climb the corporate ladder, Extroversion was crucial. Since I was good at it, it was an asset I had been convinced to hold onto and embrace. So, it was no surprise I had answered the Introversion/Extroversion portion of the questions through the lens of who other people thought I was—outgoing, social, etc.—rather than who I truly am.

A few years later (during yet another leadership course), I had another opportunity to take the MBTI and my result on the Introversion/Extroversion spectrum was much more moderate, almost right in the middle, but still technically "E." When I took the test again a few years ago, with a solid understanding of who I really am, I landed squarely on the Introvert side.

It's important to note that the Introversion/Extroversion spectrum of the MBTI doesn't tell you "what you're good at," it's intended to identify where you "get your energy from," being surrounded by people or alone with your thoughts. What builds you up and gets you excited about life? It only took me about 30 years to realize that while I was *good at* being extroverted, my energy source—who I truly am—is in fact, introverted.

The greatest realization this MBTI experience taught me was, just because I'm good at something, doesn't mean I enjoy it. Over the years, I expanded this realization all the way into my career path choices. Just because you *can* do something, doesn't mean you *have to,* or that you even *should.* Just because I'm good at herding cats and keeping organized documents of action items and project requirements, doesn't mean I like it. And even more powerful a realization, it doesn't mean I have to do it as my career.

> Just because you *can* do something, doesn't mean you *have to,* or that you even *should.*

Get Check: What skill do you continue to use or cultivate even if you don't enjoy it? Were you encouraged to develop this skill because it was something you were good at and was most likely to make you "successful"?

From our early years in elementary school, we're conditioned to be hyper-focused on our "strengths," with the ultimate goal of becoming as successful as we possibly can be, with little regard for our actual passions and interests. What things are you actually good at (i.e. business calculus as opposed to engineering calculus)? Double-down on those things and they are what you need to do with your life—*who* you need to become—because those strengths will lead you to money, power, fame, *success.* Layer on the message to Lean In so we can change the world for all of womankind and you have a solid obligation to capitalize, at all costs, on your strengths. Major in Business instead of Architecture. Find a job that leverages your extroversion because you're good at it, even though you are actually an introvert at heart.

We're so obsessed with greatness and "being successful" that we overlook what we actually *like* to do and who we truly *want* to be.

Think about your high school yearbook. If it was like every other one in America, you had a list of "Most Likelys" for the senior class. Most Likely to Become a Professional Athlete. Most Likely to Fall Asleep in Class. Most Likely to Get Detention. Most Likely to Sneak Off Campus. And of course, the highest honor of them all, Most Likely to Succeed. Interestingly, just like there are no *Working Mom* magazine covers of the average mom working an average job but living a balanced and fulfilling life, there is no "Most Likely to be Happy" in our yearbooks. Because success is what we've been told to strive for. Nothing else.

In 2001, Gallup introduced an online assessment called StrengthsFinder (since rebranded as CliftonStrengths). Its aim was to help people discover and develop their natural talents. In 2007, Gallup released the book *StrengthsFinder 2.0*, written by Tom Rath who is a renowned author and researcher in the area of human behavior. In the book, a "skill" is defined as something that can be learned and a "strength" as something one is naturally good at. My problem with these definitions is that neither account for what the individual actually *enjoys* or is passionate about. The assumption is that people automatically enjoy the things they are good at. I, too, was under this assumption during my childhood and into my early career. It's how I ended up with a very acceptable corporate job that I was good at and that paid well but did nothing for my soul. This is how millions of us end up in such situations, pursuing things we might be good at but that we don't actually care about.

Gallup's study concludes that rather than focusing efforts on improving one's weaknesses, one should focus on the things she or he is naturally good at. The justification for this guidance is that we are more likely to be "successful in life" by honing the things we are good at rather than spending energy trying to get better at things we are not.

At first brush, this is a completely reasonable argument. Rath often uses an example of a student who comes home with a report card with grades of A, C and F. Gallup conducted a study using this scenario, where parents were asked which grade needed the most attention. American participants largely answered that the F needed the most attention (supporting the study's finding that we tend to focus our efforts on improving the things we're not good at). Rath and his team argue that the

A should really be the focus and that subject matter should be cultivated in that student, because that is where that young person is most likely to be successful in life.

Now, in a perfect world, that A would be in a subject which the student also happens to be passionate about and enjoy (and I believe this is Rath's assumption). But what if it's not? What if the student gets As in all of her business courses but they are not at all interesting to her?

Our decisions and choices don't have to be guided by what's most likely to lead to success. In fact, that could be a very misleading guidepost.

As shown in Image 2, I would revise the definition to state that a "skill" is something you're good at—either naturally *or learned*—while a "strength" is something you're good at *and passionate about*.

In my own journey, I followed StrengthsFinder 2.0's guidance. My skills in architecture did not come naturally. So, when I discovered my natural skills for business, in accordance with StrengthsFinder2.0's guidance, that was my strength and therefore became my focused path.

Alternatively, if I had given my passion for architecture more consideration and realized it was okay to continue working towards something I wasn't naturally good at, even if I had to struggle to learn it, I might have stayed on my path towards architecture.

I'm still on a journey to find my own Strength... something I am good at *and I am passionate about*. Maybe it's a career change from corporate businesswoman to professional writer.

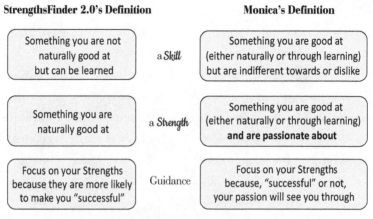

StrengthsFinder 2.0's Definition   **Monica's Definition**

StrengthsFinder 2.0's Definition		Monica's Definition
Something you are not naturally good at but can be learned	a *Skill*	Something you are good at (either naturally or through learning) but are indifferent towards or dislike
Something you are naturally good at	a *Strength*	Something you are good at (either naturally or through learning) **and are passionate about**
Focus on your Strengths because they are more likely to make you "successful"	Guidance	Focus on your Strengths because, "successful" or not, your passion will see you through

Image 2 – What About Passion?

Maybe it's simply being a great mom and wife. The point is, I've changed my focus from the pursuit of things that are most likely to make me "successful" with no regard for my passion, to the pursuit of things that will make me fulfilled, while making just enough money to provide for my family.

Maybe if I'd had this perspective earlier on, I would now be a mediocre architect making a modest living doing something I was passionate about. While I don't regret the path I've taken as it's made me who I am today, I continue to search for that passion that I had as a little girl, sitting in my room drawing mansions and RVs.

Gut Check: If "success" by society's definition weren't an issue, would you still be in the career you're in today? What did you dream of being when you were a little kid? If you never gave that dream a shot, would you still like to?

The terms "greatness," "success," and "happiness" are subjective. For those of us who live day in and day out in corporate America, that's hard to remember because everywhere we turn it seems like these things are only met by one standard formula. But once I started seeing that "successful" doesn't always have to mean a secure corporate salary, "greatness" can be defined by things other than a fancy title, and "happiness" is usually achieved separately from any professional accomplishments, I realized that my "good enough" might actually be far better than the "greatness" I had been pursuing.

Chapter 3 *Corporate Culture*

"The reward for conformity is that everyone likes
you but yourself."

- Rita Mae Brown

The corporate world is a great place for those who want to
make their career their immortality project. There are plenty
of respectable corporations with rewarding work who honestly
pursue the goal of delivering value to their customers.

But what if you've made something other than your career
your immortality project? Then corporate America is not such
an enjoyable place. One fellow Lean-Outer who is a former
registered nurse and now a stay-at-home-mom said it best when
sharing her own experience. She commented in my Instagram
community, "Every meeting with a supervisor was about what
my professional goals were for the next month, year, whatever.
And all I ever wanted to answer was 'to be able to quit this job
so I can stay home full time.' But I was constantly asked to do
more, work more, seek more opportunities, even when I had
made it clear that I was not looking for that level of commitment
at the time. All of this was from women. Successful women,

driven women, powerful women, some with children, some without [children] or with adult children. When I talked about wanting to be a SAHM, I was met by co-workers with examples of how flexible my job could be or an 'Oh, I could never do that. I'd be too bored/annoyed by my kids,' etc. Am I grateful to have the opportunities I have? Absolutely. Am I glad that if I needed/wanted to, I could go back to work and have as much right to be there as my male counterparts? No question. Do I wish that, growing up, I had been taught that raising my kids was just as valuable and fulfilling as working outside the home? Also Yes." - @briqberry

A Façade of Importance

Milo described the concept of excess and how pursuing more than we need can be attributed to our primal instincts to survive and provide. In *The Denial of Death*, Becker also shares a version of this perspective when he boils down everything we do to our innate desire to give our life meaning and find something to do all day while we sit here on this giant rock hurtling through space for the 100 years that we're alive.

Corporate America is one of the greatest examples of this importance we've created for ourselves. It's built upon customs and bureaucracies made up of inflated self-importance. It demonstrates Milo's explanation of our desire to channel our human urges to fight for survival, the extra, unnecessary effort he described as "waste" and "inefficiency."

We humans have made up this thing called "work" to give ourselves a sense of purpose, to feel like our life has meaning.

In other words, we humans have made up this thing called "work" to give ourselves a sense of purpose, to feel like our life has meaning, to have an outlet for our human urges to compete for survival, and just simply so we have something to do all day.

For those who find intrinsic fulfillment in their work and those who've chosen to make their career their immortality project, the work is not a false sense of importance. It is truly important for them. But for those of us who have chosen immortality projects other than our jobs, the corporate environment does not serve this purpose for us. As a result, most of the pomp and circumstance touted by corporate America is hard to tolerate for those of us who are here to simply do our job and go home and don't care about titles, goal setting, or quarterly reports. As described in Briana's earlier account, to those of us whose career is not our immortality project, these daily practices often seem wasteful, as a number of them seem to exist simply to make the participants give importance to the tasks they are doing, often an inflated level of importance for what the work truly is.

In 2017, a video by YouTube duo Tripp & Tyler went viral. It's called *A Conference Call in Real Life* and it depicts all the cliché technological errors, corporate jargon, and faux pas of a modern-day conference call that we're all too familiar with in the business world. While many people's favorite part is the dog barking in the background or the guy who gets dropped from the call and is shown standing outside in the hallway talking to the wall, my favorite part is a less memorable but oh-so-powerful one.

In wrapping up the meeting, the facilitator is reiterating action items and next steps and says to one co-worker, "Beth, you'll send out a recap email that could have basically taken place of this whole meeting, correct?" Beth smiles and says,

"Yep! Always do!" It's so subtle but so accurately demonstrates the waste that is commonplace in the corporate environment, as well as the façade of importance that many people work so hard to create via a vast buildup of meetings, processes, procedures, policies, email, all of which are more effective at making the participants feel like they're accomplishing something than actually being productive.

Beth's email comment is the funniest, most relatable part to me because it demonstrates precisely how wasteful the corporate world is, and how much of the daily busyness created by its participants is built simply to make the tasks seem more important than they are.

Even if your immortality project is something other than your career, when you live in this corporate world day in and day out, you end up feeling pressured to buy into these practices. Everyone around you seems to be clamoring for the external approval, via promotions and other forms of recognition. If you don't buy in, you feel like you're the odd one out and something must be wrong with you that you just can't muster up the strength to care about these things. So, as a form of self-preservation, those of us in Group H end up *pretending* that we care, going along with the mainstream and often doing such a good job that we even convince ourselves of the importance of what we're doing. The danger is that this inflated importance can end up overshadowing things that we truly do find important, our actual immortality projects.

One afternoon in the Palo Alto office of the software startup, our Business Operations team was sitting in a glass conference room discussing the professional services organization we supported and the role we should play as the organization evolved. It was a very in depth, strategic conversation that would greatly impact the future of our team. Our Director, Alex, was at the whiteboard, facilitating and driving our strategic thinking. She was smart, strong, and also warm and human. With two young kids of her own and just a few years my senior, she was exactly who I wanted to be in my own career. She seemingly "had it all," although now I see she perhaps had just figured out how to pretend she cared about Leaning In and was doing it well enough that she had everyone convinced, possibly even herself.

In the middle of a riveting point being made by a senior manager on our team, Alex got a phone call. She glanced at her phone, but rather than setting it back down as expected, her face changed, and she quickly stepped out of the room. Our team continued the conversation without her, someone else stepping up to the whiteboard. I glanced through the glass conference room walls across the open office space to see Alex talking on the phone while briskly walking back to her desk. As she talked, her face still with that same serious look I hadn't really seen before, she gathered up her laptop and purse. I watched her head to the stairwell in the back corner of the office, presumably because she didn't want to run into anyone in the elevator and feel obligated to stop to exchange pleasantries.

Alex called us from the road during her hour-long drive home and told us her four-year-old son's preschool had called. He had fallen off the play structure and possibly broken his arm, so the school's staff were taking him to urgent care. We all assured her we would continue our meeting in her absence and fill her in later. Not to worry... we supported her prioritizing her role as Mom in that moment.

Up until the moment her phone rang, Alex would have said she was doing something very important - leading her

team in a strategic conversation that would impact the future
of our department and, in turn, her career at our company and
overall.

> When your true immortality project shows up in the midst of something you often pretend is your immortality project, your true immortality project always prevails.

But when your true immortality project shows up in the midst of something you often pretend is your immortality project, your true immortality project always prevails. It's often these moments that make us realize just how silly the things we've been prioritizing actually are. Even though Alex's family emergency was not that dire or uncommon, it was still much more important to her that she be with her son in that moment than in the meeting.

I had another similar brush with perspective a few years ago on an early December morning. I was sitting at my desk on a conference call when Michael texted me that his best friend, Kevin, had just been in a car accident. Still half-listening to the conference call, I pulled up social media to find out more about our friend and the situation. Just a few minutes later, Michael called to tell me he had spoken to Kevin's wife (also a dear friend of ours) and the situation was pretty bad. Michael had already left work and was on his way home to grab a few things and then head south to be with his friends. For the rest of that afternoon, as Michael drove to potentially say good-bye to his best friend, I continued getting emails and IMs from co-workers about the daily happenings of our business. They, of course, had no idea what was going on in my world and in the lives of our friends just a few hundred miles away.

I distinctly remember reading those emails... "urgent" requests for support on a client project, formatting a report or editing a PowerPoint, and thinking, "People! Kevin might not be *alive* in a few hours. And you're worried about some stupid report?!" Again, perspective.

While Alex's story of her son's broken arm is fairly common, Kevin's story of such life-changing drama is quite rare. But either way, if you keep such perspective in the back of your mind, it most definitely impacts your overall view of your job. Not only do we maintain perspective about the importance of our work in the "grand scheme of things," but having such perspective forces us to be very deliberate about where we spend our time.

Some jobs *are* a matter of life or death, such as 911 operators, firefighters, police officers, ER doctors. And there are other professions that aren't life-and-death but have an obvious, direct impact on the lives of many, such as teachers. Even those of us in the corporate world can have very impactful jobs. Sometimes a meeting that runs late *is* more important than a kid's soccer game. Or an email *does* in fact need to be sent at 11 p.m. at night.

But even if your job is extremely impactful and fulfilling, that doesn't mean you have to *always* put it first before your family or other priorities. At the very worst, if you struggle to find intrinsic fulfillment in your work and you're not motivated by external motivators such as promotions or raises, then you are probably motivated by simply not losing your job. Now, if this is all that's keeping you going, then you might want to think about finding a new job. But, at the very root of it, isn't this the most basic motivator for all of us? Aren't we working to earn a paycheck so that we can buy food to feed ourselves

and our young? Aren't we all just cavemen who are out hunting
and gathering, bringing home our latest "kill" in the form of a
corporate salary and benefits?

If you look at it from this very stripped-down, human
perspective, where keeping your job so you can feed your
family is your main motivator, then there will be times when
you have to put your job before your family, just to keep your
job, so that you can feed your family. Ironic, right?

But these are case-by-case decisions. Yes, sometimes a
work meeting is more important than your child's soccer game.
But this doesn't mean meetings are *always* more important.
It doesn't mean your *overall career* has to come before raising
your family. This is the distinction we need to make very clear.
There will always be times when something at work actually
needs to be prioritized. But that doesn't have to mean that work
is *always* more important. This is the key difference between
the Lean In perspective which, in order to reach leadership
levels, requires you to view your career as a constant matter of
life and death, and the Lean Out perspective which encourages
honest evaluation of your job's importance in the context of
your broader life. Don't give your job more importance than
it actually has.

How Perspective Affects Ambition

When I was pregnant with my first son, I had persistent
nausea. I never actually threw up the whole 40 weeks, but
I *felt* like I was about to throw up, the entire pregnancy.
At the time I was working at Lockheed Martin in a project
management role.

One morning, sitting in a tiny, stuffy conference room
where the dirty, beige 40-year-old carpet blended right into

the beige 40-year-old walls of faux wood paneling, a handful of us were discussing a military satellite communications proposal we were going to submit to the US Air Force. It was an important project for our business and a fairly crucial meeting. But that room was so stuffy. It was all I could do to not lean over the table and hurl, let alone focus on the topic at hand and contribute anything of value.

The meeting was running over its scheduled time and creeping into the 20 minute block of time I had between meetings that day, during which I had planned to grab lunch so that my unborn child could keep growing, and I could keep from hurling all over everyone.

I could feel the nausea worsening by the minute as my stomach became emptier. I needed to eat something and quick. Not just to prevent the nausea but to feed the tiny human growing inside of me. So, the next chance I had to interject, I politely excused myself by playing the pregnancy card and sharing my situation. They all quickly made space for me and my oversized belly to squeeze past them and out of that hellhole of a conference room.

My purely biological need to eat imposed a sense of perspective that has remained with me to this day. It changed my entire outlook on "work" and "my career." I realized that it's impossible to care about formatting a proposal when you're about to hurl. Even when dealing with something like a multi-billion-dollar government contract, nothing seems as important as growing a human life inside of you. And this perspective stuck with me when years later I realized it's hard to care about answering one more email on your laptop on the couch at home when your child is gently patting your hand, sweetly asking, "Mama, *now* can you play with me?"

When I was pregnant, eating was more important than a meeting. And my job didn't go back to being more important than my children once they were born. If anything, the distinct priorities solidified even more. During my first years as a mother, there were many small but significant shifts where I forwent the traditional external approval I would've typically sought and instead chose intrinsic fulfillment through my role as a wife and mother. I stopped pretending my career was my immortality project and embraced my new one of raising my children.

I had less interest in the happy hours and stretch assignments... things I used to gladly participate in to make me stand out from my peers and earn even more external approval. I just wanted to get home to my family.

I read fewer "kick in the pants" memoirs and "how to climb the ladder" books by successful businesswomen and instead found myself drawn more to stories about parenting and balance. My perfectly blow-dried and straightened hair gave way to the messy bun - thanks to the toddler I now had to get up and out the door by 6:30 a.m. each morning. And, thanks in large part to my postpartum body, my sleek pant suits and pencil skirts were traded in for black stretch pants and comfy blouses.

All of the challenges and happenings at work that used to seem so important, no longer were. I still did my job and did it well, but all the spreadsheets and PowerPoints, all the product launches and user conferences, everything just paled in comparison to my role as a mom. I realized that nothing I ever do professionally will be more important or more impactful than the job I have raising three human beings.

Mother Theresa has been quoted as having said, "If you want to change the whole world, go home and love your family." And this is exactly what I realized when my immortality project shifted from professional "greatness" to prioritizing my job as a mom.

Nothing I ever do professionally will be more important or more impactful than the job I have raising three human beings.

Gut Check: Do you have a healthy perspective on the importance of your job in relation to your immortality project and the broader world we live in? Have you fallen into the trap of assigning false importance to the inconsequential tasks of the corporate world?

Addiction to External Approval

As a society, we tend to look down on those who pursue their passions: the wide-eyed aspiring actor who moves from the Midwest to Hollywood in hopes of becoming a star, the so-so architect who turned down an alternative career path of professional prestige to instead follow her passion. We label them as "dreamers" or judge their behavior to be irresponsible. Instead, we expect those who've been blessed with education and opportunity to be singularly focused on pursuit of that holy grail of "greatness" and "success."

This is especially true for us Xennial and Millennial girls. From a very early age, we felt we owed it to the women who came before us to do something amazing in our lives. Not only were we grateful to them, we were obligated to achieve, to honor all they had done for us. After all, they had sacrificed so much and fought so hard. It would be an awful waste if we didn't seize all the opportunities we were fortunate to have.

As a result, instead of making our life's purpose personal fulfillment, we make it the approval of others. We strive to

> Instead of making our life's purpose personal fulfillment, we make it the approval of others.

show others that we did the most we could with the opportunities we've been blessed with.

Furthermore, it seems like the need for external approval is higher when someone's immortality project is one that is measurable and open for evaluation by others. In the corporate world your level of success is easily – and regularly – measured by your title and the amount of money you make. Those of us who live in this world know all too well the constant performance reviews, calibration meetings, and career discussions. They're all constant reminders and evaluations of "how we're doing." On the other hand, raising your children is a much more private immortality project. In general, no one other than your family is thinking about how good of a job you're doing as a parent. It's really up to you to determine how you feel about the "success" of your immortality project.

If your immortality project is a more private one, you can look towards your own intrinsic fulfillment rather than external approval to give you a sense of "how you're doing." This is why for people like me and @briqberry whose reflections I shared earlier, the "traditions" of corporate America can seem so forced and unnecessary. They are pastimes we came up with to busy ourselves and make our lives feel meaningful. As individuals whose careers aren't our immortality projects, we don't care about these things. And it's exhausting to pretend to. This is where the systems and structures of the corporate world break down because, like Sheryl Sandberg and the Lean In message, they incorrectly assume that everyone's immortality project is their career.

During my last week at Lockheed Martin, I remember being asked what I would miss most about working there, after almost 10 years of dutiful "service." I answered that I'd miss "the work significance," a phrase that had become very handy when I managed the company's intern program and tried desperately to attract top talent from Silicon Valley neighbors like Apple, Google and some new thing called Facebook. We claimed that the work we did directly saved lives and defended our country, which is definitely true for a defense contractor like Lockheed Martin. But in my case, what I now realize I really meant when I said I'd miss the work significance was, "I'll miss the external approval I get when I tell people I work for Lockheed Martin and they respond with admiration and approval."

It wasn't the actual work that I was intrinsically proud of, seeing as how I'd never designed or touched, barely even *seen* a piece of actual hardware or product in my nearly 10 years there. And while my work in different business functions was valued and appreciated by my co-workers, it was never intrinsically fulfilling for me. What I was really going to miss was the approval I got from strangers when I spoke about being at Cape Canaveral for a satellite launch, something that sounded much more impressive than the role I actually played there... handing out t-shirts and stickers.

Leaving the juggernaut defense contractor in Sunnyvale for a small software startup just 20 minutes across town in Palo Alto, I may as well have been traveling to another planet. At Lockheed, it had been all about 50-year-old government programs, policy and procedure, the US and Ally Defense budgets, and Top Secret clearances. At my new company, it was all about rounds of funding, elevator pitches, free food and ping pong tournaments. The kid at the desk next to me had a two-drawer filing cabinet. He had made some makeshift labels out of Post-Its and Scotch tape. The top drawer he had labeled as "Top Secret." The bottom drawer he had labeled, "Bottom Secret." It perfectly summed up the stark contrast between the cold bureaucracy I had left behind and the exuberant chaos I had entered. Hopefully, I'd finally be able to find some intrinsic fulfillment here and, with two beautiful babies at home, I'd be able to "have it all"; intrinsic fulfillment at home and in my job.

Fortunately for my then external approval-addicted self, I soon discovered that telling people I worked at the software startup that was backed by the same VC firm that had backed Google meant I received just as many nods of approval as I had working for the huge defense contractor.

But over the following months and years, as my immortality project shifted from corporate ladder climbing to raising children, I cared less and less about what others thought of my professional title or the name of my employer. I rotated through a number of positions in from human resources to program management to business development and marketing, all attempts to find intrinsic fulfillment in my job similar to that I'd come to know in my role as a mom. I no longer cared about a specific job's career progression, earning potential, or how people would react when I told them the name of the company I worked for. I just wanted to find work that was challenging, leveraged my strengths, and was fulfilling - just as I had found motherhood to be. I needed to earn enough to pay the bills and give my kids the life that Michael and I agreed to be appropriate – but nothing more.

I had always hoped that one of these times when I started a new role with a new company, I would magically have a sudden rush of ambition to Lean Into the job and rise to the very top of that organization, out of pure passion for the work or my own personal pursuit of accomplishment.

As much as I enjoy growing my skillset, building relationships with co-workers, and making a comfortable living for my family, I've just never been able to muster up a desire to pursue more than that.

I've never felt compelled to go out of my way to do everything I can for my employer, especially at the cost of my personal priorities. Even though I've been told my whole life that I have "leadership potential." I've never felt an internal urge to seek leadership opportunities purely for the sake of leading others.

Like most women who find themselves in such a position, I've always chalked up this lack of ladder-climbing ambition to the excuses we usually hear: I supposedly lack confidence, I need mentoring, I'm being held back because I'm a woman, or I have too much to juggle so I can't hack it. Although I always knew in my heart none of these explanations were true for me, they were the socially agreed-upon reasons why women like me don't Lean Into their careers. So, I sought mentors, I looked for stretch assignments, I did what I was supposed to do to overcome this "evil" block I had in my professional ambition, since it was apparently a negative thing that meant something was wrong with me.

Since my immortality project eventually become raising my children—one that was not considered as "success" for a woman of my education and opportunities—I continued trying to gain external approval via these corporate accomplishments, by Leaning Into my career and trying to climb the ladder, since

it seemed that was what society would value me for (as we saw
Glenn Close's speech allude to). Eventually, when my desire
for intrinsic fulfillment outweighed my desire for external
approval, I stopped needing it so much. In fact, I realized it
had come to be a sort of addiction and one that I was realizing
I wanted to beat.

Fortunately, I don't have much personal experience with
drug addiction. But through my own process of changing
immortality projects from my career to raising my children,
caring less about external approval and instead seeking
intrinsic fulfillment, I noticed how similar my relationship
with external approval has been to that of an addiction.

Exposure - I learned at an early age of the "high"
I could get from pleasing others. While I wasn't a naturally
gifted student, I worked hard to earn decent grades and,
more importantly, I followed the rules. You could say I was
the teacher's pet: always volunteering to lead a group activity,
speak in front of the class, clean up or perform other chores
to help out the teacher. While the favor of adults didn't make
me one of the "cool kids" (a route to validation that is more
common), the kudos I got from my teachers and parents for
being a "good kid" was extremely satisfying.

Addiction - When I graduated college, I moved right
into corporate America, a place where external approval was
being sold on every proverbial street corner. From leadership
development programs to stellar performance reviews to
president's awards, what started out as a "bad habit" soon
became my full-blown addiction. The validation I received was
addicting. The more I got, the more I craved.

Corporate America basically became my dealer. In this
environment, many become so addicted that they will do

anything for the drug. Whether it's miss their kid's soccer game for a last-minute work meeting or spend hours at night responding to emails that aren't really urgent. The next morning, they get their "fix" when their boss gives them a pat on the back for making it to the meeting or when their peers read that 2 a.m. email and respond "Wow! Burning that midnight oil, eh?" But what about the kid whose soccer game they missed? What about the spouse who sat alone on the couch while the addict worked all night? Just like a drug addiction, these people and these relationships are impacted in a very real way.

The high you get from external approval keeps you in a vicious loop of practicing this unhealthy behavior of sacrificing things that are truly important to you.

> The high you get from external approval keeps you in a vicious loop of practicing this unhealthy behavior of sacrificing things that are truly important to you.

The irony is that the "high" you could get from those truly important things (time with family, exercise, hobbies, SLEEP) is usually an even *better* high in the long run than that of external approval. But if you're addicted to something, you can't see past the addiction that's right in front of you, even if something better exists on the other side. This is why millions of people get trapped in over-commitments to their jobs.

While our society claims that these other things like family are important, there is no public recognition (or external approval) for them. There's no *Top 30 under 30* honoring the best moms in America who are raising exceptional human beings. There are no Hollywood actresses giving acceptance speeches about how parenthood, too, can be a great accomplishment.

No, in our society, such public recognition is only obtained through professional success - either through an impressive title, money, or fame. So, if you've been conditioned like most of us have to crave external approval, these are the things you will spend your time and energy seeking; pursuing that "high" you've become so addicted to. The corporate world also encourages this behavior by masking the addiction with fancy, admirable-sounding terms like "Lean In," so it's even easier to justify the addiction.

What's worse, if you overcommit to your job while pursuing such things, then your personal and home life will start to suffer. Once your personal and home life start suffering, you will want to escape or avoid them all together. You'll actually *prefer* to stay at work where you'll get a bunch of external approval because you're "working so hard," rather than face the disappointments in your personal life. It's a vicious spiral that is nearly impossible to escape.

For the first 10 years of my career, I was as addicted as the next girl. I wanted to climb the corporate ladder as high as I possibly could, not because I was avoiding anything in my personal life but simply because each new rung I climbed gave me a huge hit of external approval. Each promotion, each pay raise, each moment of public recognition in an all-hands meeting, each time I told a stranger what I did for work and got a nod of approval, it all gave me a great rush. I thought I intrinsically wanted these things but, in hindsight, it was just the hits of external approval that came along with them.

At the height of my addiction I became a mother, which I now realize literally saved my life. I discovered an alternative source which gave me an even greater high than external approval: the *intrinsic fulfillment* I got from being a good parent.

Still, my addiction to external approval was deeply entrenched and did not disappear overnight. For a while I tried to have it both ways (what our society has nicknamed "having it all": external approval from meeting corporate America's expectations *and* intrinsic fulfillment from taking care of your family). But the more I tried to have both, the more I realized it was impossible. Not because of some logistical challenges like time management. But because it's a complete contradiction to try to simultaneously pursue external approval in one area of your life and intrinsic fulfillment in another.

Withdrawals - After the birth of my second and third child, my intrinsic fulfillment continued to reduce my need for external approval until it was practically gone. I wanted to let go of my old addiction entirely and just bathe in the greater fulfillment of my new immortality project. But first I had to go through a period of "withdrawals" from my old addiction to external approval. This withdrawal manifested itself in the most unexpected way that I'll describe more later on.

Living Clean - As a recovering addict still living with my corporate world "dealer" amongst many other "addicts," I have to consciously make the right choices and say, "No," to external approval every day. I must focus on the intrinsic fulfilment in my personal and professional life, even when—*especially* when—that means foregoing a hit of external approval. I find it helpful to have many "sponsors" in my life who also value intrinsic fulfillment over external approval and accept the fact that I'm no longer pursuing society's definition of success.

Gut Check: Are you addicted to external approval? Or perhaps going through a period of "withdrawals" trying to not need it anymore? What steps can you take to beat your addiction?

Fake It 'til You Make It

There's a popular phrase amongst our community of professional women, specifically in the corporate world: "fake it 'til you make it." It's intended to address the sensation felt by women who secretly feel they aren't qualified to be in the position they are in, referred to as "imposter syndrome." Personally, I've never suffered from this imposter syndrome because I began Leaning Out of my career before I climbed far enough out of my comfort zone and away from my true self.

> If you have to "fake it 'til you make it," then maybe "it" isn't who you really are.

But I have a different take on this expression. If you have to "fake it 'til you make it," then maybe "it" isn't who you really are. If you don't feel comfortable rising up the corporate ladder, whether it's due to a lack of confidence or because you feel you have to hide the fact that you're a mother whose true immortality project is your children, then maybe you shouldn't be rising up the ladder.

Again, there's a huge distinction between those who truly *do* want to climb the ladder and aren't faking anything. Climb on, girlfriend. But for those of us whose gut is telling us "This isn't you," maybe our gut is on to something. Let's stop faking like our career is our immortality project if it's really not.

Reflecting on my own journey and the decision I've intentionally made to not climb the ladder, this expression makes me wonder if some women who suffer from imposter syndrome do so because the positions and jobs they find themselves in are not true to who they really are. Maybe they're in such a position because they kept climbing the ladder out of some obligation to do so, not because it's what they actually wanted.

For this reason, I would give "fake it 'til you make it" a new meaning. As opposed to a way of combating imposter syndrome which claims we lack the confidence to be where we are, I think that for many of us, "fake it 'til you make it" is really about pretending your career is your immortality project, until you've convinced everyone - even yourself - that it actually is.

> "Fake it 'til you make it" is really about pretending your career is your immortality project.

What this expression says to me is, if you're actually an Introvert but you're good at acting Extroverted, then pretend you're an Extrovert until you actually become one. If you're good at Business but don't really enjoy it, just pretend you enjoy it until you actually do. If who you really aren't going to cut it, pretend you're someone else until you become someone else.

Don't get me wrong. I have no problem with giving yourself a pep talk every once in a while. We can all benefit from a little confidence boost, if that in fact is the root problem. My concern is when you are behaving in a way, or pursuing a career path that is so far from what you actually want—who you actually are—that you have to put on an act, you have to convince others and even yourself that it's real.

If you've found yourself in a role that is impressive on paper, but you look in the mirror at the pantsuit-wearing, ladder-climbing, Leaning In career woman, and you have to convince yourself that the person you see is in fact you, that she really is who you want to be, then maybe it's time to stop faking.

Along these lines, there's another related phrase that's constantly pitched to professional working women: "dress for success." If you think about it, it's the visual embodiment of "fake it 'til you make it." It implies that, if you dress a certain way, people are more likely to believe you are the person who you're trying so hard to convince them (and yourself) that you are. You're more likely to be taken seriously, to be valued, and to be considered for promotion.

I can't argue with the fact that, as human creatures we make judgements about others based on their physical appearance. Extensive research has been conducted in this area which has confirmed that taller people are more likely to be listened to or viewed as leaders. When it comes to dress, I agree that the way people dress in corporate culture does in fact change how others view them. Actors use costumes to help them get into character (convince themselves that they are who they're pretending to be) and to make their performance even more authentic to their audience. And that's exactly what we're doing when we "dress for success" at work. We're trying to convince ourselves and others of who we're trying to be.

If you're someone who simply enjoys dressing up, then good for you. If you don't intrinsically enjoy it but truly want to be CEO and therefore feel it's important to dress like one every day, then go ahead. But for me, when I worked in an office where jeans and t-shirts were the norm, that's what you found me in.

Of course, I don't expect the entire professional world to wake up tomorrow and decide to get rid of professional attire in favor of comfort. But if it wasn't all a charade, why then do we place so much importance on our appearance and "dressing for success?"

When you picture Facebook CEO and billionaire, Mark Zuckerberg, what do you picture him wearing? Jeans and a hoodie, right? Now what about his female counterpart and COO—our fearless Lean In leader—Sheryl Sandberg?

In every public appearance and even on the cover of *Lean In*, she's in a classy pantsuit with perfectly coiffed hair. On Casual Fridays at the Facebook office, I'm told she can be found in nice jeans and flats, but likely with a blouse or blazer. And even on the few occasions she might be found in a hoodie with a messy bun, this is the exception and it isn't the image she wants us to associate with her. It won't be on the cover of her next book. No, her brand of "successful businesswoman" is associated with the famous image of her in a classy pantsuit and perfect hair, just like Zuckerberg is known for his hoodie and jeans.

If you've been "dressing for success" and "faking it trying to make it" for many years (like I had been), the process of Leaning Out or right-sizing your life that we'll talk about in chapter four can be a hard one, and can take time. In many cases, we've been "faking it" for so long that we've convinced even *ourselves* that we are the person we see in the mirror. Getting back to who we truly are and discovering who we truly want to be is easier said than done.

But for now, if you've been suffering from imposter syndrome, think about why that might be. Is it due to a lack of confidence or might it be because you're trying to "fake it" and be someone you just aren't? Do you really want to be a Director or VP? Is that woman in the mirror with the sharp pantsuit and perfect haircut the real you? If your answer is yes, then great. But if your answer is no and you're tired of "faking it," start being honest with yourself.

Gut Check: Have you been "faking it trying to make it?" What exactly are you faking? *Why* are you doing it? Are you tired of faking? What would your life look like if you began living more authentically to who you truly are?

What Would Anne Hathaway Do?

In the 2006 movie, *The Devil Wears Prada*, Anne Hathaway's character, Andy, is a bright-eyed aspiring journalist who lands a dream job working as assistant to the editor in chief of a renowned fashion magazine. Although Andy is extremely good at the impossibly demanding job and is surprised to find how much she enjoys the recognition and praise from her uber-judgy boss, it starts to affect her relationships with her friends, boyfriend and most importantly, herself. In many ways she is "faking it 'til she makes it," putting up a façade that she wants this high-stress, high-profile career when internally something about it doesn't feel right. She even "dresses for success," as the movie is famous for all the stylish outfits and glamour Andy adopts in her effort to "fake it."

Towards the climax of the movie, Andy starts to realize that she doesn't like who she has become even though, by all standards, she is on the fast-track to success and could have anything she wants professionally speaking. Counter to messages like *Lean In*, Andy decides to exit her fast track to money and power and instead walks away with her priorities and convictions.

In the final scene where she meets her estranged boyfriend to apologize and tell him that she's seen the error of her ways, she is noticeably back to wearing her average clothing, having shed the "costume" of designer dresses and handbags she had been wearing when she was Leaning Into her career. The audience cries tears of joy for the young woman, hoping that we, too, would make the hard decision to reject success and external approval, and opt instead for a life of intrinsic fulfillment and balance.

Nine years later, in 2015, Hathaway hit us again with a similar message starring opposite Robert DeNiro in *The*

Intern. Her character, Jules, is a self-made woman and CEO of her own company (an online fashion service - leading me to believe that *The Intern* is secretly the sequel to *The Devil Wears Prada*). At the peak of its growth, Jules' company is flourishing. She seems to "have it all" and is like CEO Chick, sporting heels and trench coat while jaunting down a city street. But in reality, Jules' life is a mess. Her marriage that she thought was rock-solid turns out to be crumbling in a directly inverse relationship to her professional trajectory. She doesn't even enjoy her job any more for many reasons. Luckily, she has an opportunity to step down as CEO, but even though she wants to, she is reluctant to let go of the professional success that she's become so reliant on to find her fulfillment.

Our knee-jerk reaction is to call Jules' hesitation "imposter syndrome," blaming her desire to Lean Out on a lack of confidence or some intimidating male superior. But she doesn't lack confidence. In fact, she feels obligated to stay on as CEO because she knows no one else could run her company as well as she could. What is actually causing her hesitation is her subconscious desire to put less energy into her career so she can put more into her marriage and her life.

Fortunately, the wise DeNiro character helps her understand, that it's okay for her to Lean Out, and that she isn't failing by admitting that she cares more about her family and her personal happiness than she does about her professional accomplishments. Once again, Hathaway's character inspires us all as she takes the less popular, less socially-recognized route but follows her heart, Leans Out of her career and into her family, and finds true happiness.

Beyond Hathaway's hits, the list of Hollywood rom-coms where the female protagonist has a life-changing perspective that leads her to stress less about her career and prioritize her relationships and personal life is endless.

But these stories seem contradictory to the Lean In message we're also being fed, don't they? So why is this theme so pervasive in the movies? How come you never see box office hits of a woman with a decent but unimpressive job, a happy marriage with two great kids, a well-balanced life, who then goes through a journey of self-discovery that leads her to Lean In and give more of herself to her career?

Because no one wants to see that! No one actually does that and none of us want that for ourselves. The Lean In campaign seems to think there is a mass of professional women out there enjoying balance and happiness while desiring more in our professional lives. It claims the reason we don't pursue more professionally is because exterior hurdles stand in our way.

But really, it's the other way around. Millions of us are in situations like Anne Hathaway. We've been Leaning Into our careers and are actually accomplishing quite a lot, but all the while, our personal lives and our true selves are suffering. We all secretly want a DeNiro figure to come into our lives and tell us it's okay to not want "it all," that we don't have to be CEO if we don't want to be, and we're

> We've been Leaning Into our careers and are actually accomplishing quite a lot, but all the while, our personal lives and our true selves are suffering.

not weak or a failure by admitting this to ourselves and to everyone else. This is why movies like Hathaway's are such hits... because they're speaking to millions of us who have the same secret truth.

Gut Check: If Hollywood were to make your life into a box office hit, and Anne Hathaway were to play you, what would she be grappling with? Would she take the "right" path or would she follow her heart?

"Work-Life Balance" Cliché

Recently, I was talking with a senior leader in my IT organization. She was telling me about the hard time she was having filling a crucial opening she has for an analyst position. Apparently, she had just interviewed a candidate who had a solid education, stellar experience, amazing recommendations and a decent interview all except for one part. The candidate had asked about our work culture (not an uncommon question in an interview) and, since she would be working remotely, mentioned to the leader that she would like to be able to walk her dog during the day. The leader was telling me this story out of shock and disappointment. She couldn't believe that the candidate had the gall to ask such a question! To me, I was thrilled to hear how this outstanding young woman had her priorities defined and was holding firm to her personal convictions while knowing her worth and being unwilling to settle for a position that wouldn't respect her needs.

This is exactly the kind of thing that Lean In advocates would advise this young woman against. Instead of sharing her priorities openly and honestly, Lean In culture would have her present herself as 100% committed to her work and available at all times with no priorities that could possibly interfere with her professional greatness. *Don't mention you want to walk your dog. Don't mention you have a dog at all.* But why shouldn't she be able to walk her dog during the day if she is doing her work and adding value? And as the hiring manager, why wouldn't you see this as a sign of emotional intelligence and competence in this young woman? If we all start setting firm boundaries for ourselves and respecting each other's, then the corporate world wouldn't demand such ridiculous personal sacrifice.

Despite the example of this one closed-minded manager, modern corporate culture is starting to embrace the trend of work-life balance, thanks to advances in technology and trends like the gig economy. But we have to be careful with this expression "work-life balance," or what has been rebranded as "work-life integration." Since we no longer leave work at the office, the lines between work and life are blurrier than ever. We have to be intentional about how we fit our work into our overall life. This cultural shift has made it more possible than ever to Lean Out; to manage our work in a way that suits our life. Thanks to technology, it no longer matters where on Earth we are working from or what hours we are working. Of course, this is a double-edged sword as it allows greater flexibility but also means everyone is expected to be accessible 24/7. Whether the pros outweigh the cons is up to the individual.

If you're someone who feels compelled to "log back in" at night after the kids have gone to bed, or you willingly join a conference call even if it's during your scheduled family vacation since, technically, you are able to join from your hotel room, then you're going to suffer from the "cons" of these modern advancements. You're going to feel constantly on call, always at work, always Leaning In.

In order to experience the "pros" of this flexible work culture, it is crucial to clearly define our own boundaries and hold firm to them even when the pressure to Lean In tempts us to break them (much like our friend who was firm about her need to walk her dog). More on this in chapter four.

Leaning Out is about deciding what level of investment you want to make in your career, which in turn allows you to have the level of personal life that you also want. It's a fresh take on the worn-out expression "work-life balance" where usually "work" means achieving as much as you can and "life balance" means magically squeezing in the "life" part into whatever bandwidth you have left. Instead, "work-life balance" should be about choosing the right level of mental, physical and emotional energy that you want to devote to your career and to your personal life. The possible levels of distribution between the two are infinite and dynamic and, if you choose not to dedicate all of your energy to your career, that's okay.

I've found through my own experience and that of friends and co-workers that the distribution or the "balance" you end up with is largely influenced by which side of the Work-Life spectrum you start. We will naturally dedicate most of our energy to the side of life that we prioritize or "start on". The other side just gets our leftovers. If you work in the corporate world, your employer will take all that you're willing to give. They won't "cut you off" after you've worked 50 hours that week, sending you home to see your kids and spouse who miss you. If you choose to start on the Work side, they will let you work 24/7 and dedicate all of your time and energy to your job. This is why it's dangerous to start on the Work side of the equation: it's hard to cut off how much of yourself you are willing to dedicate there.

Notice the person in the second example in Image 3 is Leaning Into their career even though it is not their immortality project. As a result, they end up with nothing but "leftovers" to spend on their immortality project. This is what is happening to so many of us in Group H. We give our time and energy first to the Work side and inevitably don't have as much energy left as we'd like to give to our immortality project on the Life side. If we instead start on the Life side as shown by the third example in Image 3, we are able to give of ourselves fully to our immortality project and Work gets our leftovers. Our leftovers are enough to still do our job if we Lean Out of working long hours that aren't necessary and stop pursuing extra responsibility and titles we don't actually want. We will no longer be climbing the ladder but instead will be able to dedicate ourselves first to our immortality project.

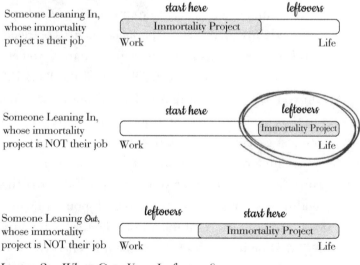

Image 3 – What Gets Your Leftovers?

Of course, there are numerous details and logistics that go into this process which we'll talk about in chapter four. But the point is, if your career is not your true immortality project, then don't start on the

> If your career is not your true immortality project, then don't start on the Work side of your balance spectrum.

Work side of your balance spectrum. If you do, you will likely expend way more time and energy there than you actually want to, leaving you with less than you'd like to have for your immortality project and other areas of your life.

In looking at this distribution of your own time and energy, you may find that you can't continue under your current circumstances. Maybe you work full time at a top law firm where you actually have to work 60 hours a week in order to perform at the level expected. Maybe as you shift which side of the equation you start on, you realize you're only left with 45 hours a week or so for your job, so you're no longer willing or able to commit to working at that firm. Maybe you can find a similar job at a different firm, or even go into business for yourself. Perhaps you work at a family-friendly company, but you're in a leadership position that eats up more emotional energy than you realize you want to spend. Perhaps you can consider stepping back into an individual contributor role, at least during this phase of your life.

It's important to clarify once again that whatever distribution a person makes between Work and Life is a personal choice. The point is to deliberately make these choices, rather than automatically accept what is offered to you. Critically consider whether or not each choice will align your life in a way that allows you to first expend your time and energy on your immortality project.

Gut Check: Have you been dedicating your time and energy to your immortality project first, or is it getting your "leftovers"?

With Great Privilege Comes Great Obligation

I grew up in Silicon Valley in the '90s. Most of the kids in my world came from homes where, not only both parents worked, but their moms had corporate careers equivalent to their dads. I never saw my future – my potential – as anything different from that of my male peers. All of us – boys and girls – were born in the right place at the right time and were all raised to Lean In and achieve professional greatness.

At this impressionable time in my life I was surrounded by opportunity and high-profile accomplishment, leading me to believe this was the only acceptable path for someone like me to follow. In high school, my classmates' parents were early Apple employees, founders of Netflix, and engineers designing new technologies like Blu-ray. Such professional success appeared to be mine for the taking. It was wonderful to have such opportunities. But at the same time, if I didn't take those opportunities, what would that say about me? 10 years later, reading on my Kindle in the mothers' room while pumping at work, I would also learn that "women around the world were counting on me" to succeed. As a white American woman with education and opportunity, I had no excuse *not* to achieve professional greatness.

As you're reading this, I'm sure the word "privilege" is coming to mind, and I wouldn't argue with the fact that I am very privileged. Having more opportunity than you want is not really a problem. I am grateful to have been born in a time and a place where this pressure to achieve was my greatest challenge. The problem is, this life path was never presented to me as a *choice* and for me, this particular path was not a good one. I was expected to want to Lean In and achieve my greatest professional potential at all costs which, for someone who wanted to make family her greatest priority, were pretty high.

As someone with such opportunity, choosing not to Lean In is viewed as being ungrateful, anti-feminist, or a failure. Deliberately choosing to be mediocre when you've been given the chance to be "great" is not acceptable in the eyes of our modern society.

> Deliberately choosing
> to be mediocre when
> you've been given the
> chance to be "great"
> is not acceptable
> in the eyes of our
> modern society.

The environment I grew up in was like that in my daughter's book that I spoke of in chapter one where society constantly asks, "How will you change the world?" as if I could only do something truly ground-breaking with my life, never asking whether or not I even *wanted to* change the world. Fortunately for me, my parents were right there beside me through childhood and into adulthood, tailoring the message by adding "you don't have to change the world to be a good person or for me to love you." Although it took a good 10 years of my early adulthood, fruitlessly pursuing what society expected of me, in the end it was my parents' example of balance and intrinsic fulfillment over external approval that eventually led me to the path that was best for me.

My mom is an extremely balanced woman who has always valued family and relationships while also pursuing a career that she loved and found intrinsically fulfilling. She was a full-time mom until my sister and I were 12 and 10 years old, at which point she went back to school to obtain her teaching credential and fulfilled her dream of becoming an elementary school teacher. Last spring, we celebrated her retirement – 25 years of teaching first and second graders how to read, write, and be decent people. But as dedicated as she was to her profession, she never missed any important events or milestones of mine or my sister's. She was never overly stressed or overwhelmed by her job. While teaching can often be a thankless job, my mom always enjoyed it and found intrinsic fulfillment in her work, but never at the cost of her family or her happiness. She understood what true balance required because she chose how much she wanted to give of herself to her work, never giving more than she was willing to, which allowed her to preserve enough time, energy and strength for her other priorities.

My dad similarly exemplifies what it is to be balanced. He started out on the fast track up the corporate ladder. In his early career with a large financial trading company, he was rewarded with accolades and financial incentives, but he found himself making personal sacrifices he didn't want to make, working long hours he didn't enjoy and, although he had all the opportunity to climb the ladder if he wanted to, he walked away from it all at the peak of his potential. For the last 25 years he has worked for himself as an independent financial advisor, helping individuals plan their finances and lead happier, more secure lives. While he makes a decent living, it is nothing compared to the wealth, titles, fancy corner offices and external approval that would have been his had he stayed with the large investment firm and continued Leaning Into that career path. Instead, he found a job he enjoyed that let him help others while still being home by 5pm every day and never working in the evenings or on weekends.

He's enjoyed a modest lifestyle, setting his own schedule and priorities, allowing him to enjoy his hobbies like playing bocce with his buddies. To this day, my parents don't even have internet service at their home! Their relaxed, unimpressive but low-pressure lifestyle would not be the case had either of my parents pursued a high-powered career in the corporate world. But for them, moderate work weeks and no internet service exemplifies the firm boundaries they've set which allow them to live a life aligned to their priorities.

This is the kind of example I have similarly chosen to set for my own children; someone who works hard but does not set their priorities according to what others think they should be. Society might tell my children that they need to pursue money, power, fame, and greatness in their field to be valued, but as long as their mom and dad regularly correct that message with our words and our example, I'm confident my children will find the right path for themselves, just as I did.

Gut Check: What type of example do you want to set for your children? Are your priorities and current lifestyle aligned to that example?

The obligation to Lean In while secretly wishing we could Lean Out is more than just a personal dilemma for a few. The problem is that it is socially unacceptable for women to express out loud that all we want is a decent job while being able to prioritize other aspects of our lives.

It is socially unacceptable for women to express out loud that all we want is a decent job while being able to prioritize other aspects of our lives.

While women without the level of education or formal experience to qualify them for a professional career are respected as stay-at-home-mothers, if someone with professional credentials chooses to be a stay-at-home-mother (like Briana did) or continue working but deliberately remain in middle management rather than ascend to a high-powered position (like I've done), we are viewed as failures or disappointments, falling short of our potential and letting down all of womankind.

As a result, even if we don't actually *want* that promotion with the additional responsibility, we begrudgingly accept it anyway because we feel obligated to pursue that raise, that title, that additional power. Because as human creatures, we're programmed to strive to be "the best" in order to survive. Add to this the fact that, according to Sheryl Sandberg, "women all around the world are counting on us," and it's no wonder why we all feel so obligated to Lean In!

So if you're a woman who has found intrinsic fulfillment in raising little human beings, who has let go of her pursuit for external approval, who has no time or patience for the B.S. of the corporate world, and who sees right through the "façade of importance" that others are desperately trying to hold up to support their own immortality project, it's no surprise you have no desire to Lean Into that world. And that's perfectly okay. Let's talk about what you can do instead.

Part II

What We Can Do About It

Chapter 4 *For Ourselves*

"We have overstretched our personal boundaries and forgotten that true happiness comes from living an authentic life fueled with a sense of purpose and balance."

- Oprah Winfrey

When my oldest son Tommy was about 19 months old, I went on my first major business trip since becoming a mom. It was to be a week-long trip to Florida, to support the marketing and events during Lockheed's launch of a satellite at Cape Canaveral. The events, which I had been a part of planning for months in advance, all went off without a hitch. The few hundred executive leaders from my company and high-ranking military officials in attendance all looked to me to tell them where to be, what to say, which bus to get on and who to shake hands with. It was very exciting and memorable... an experience I will always treasure. Unfortunately, the day of the launch, as we all watched and listened from our posts around the Cape, we ended up waiting for a few extra hours and eventually the launch was called off due to adverse weather (not uncommon when launching a rocket into space). We soon found out that the launch would be attempted again in 24 hours. Until then, our team was expected to just sit tight and hang around Cape Canaveral.

The new launch day was to be Michael's 33rd birthday. And while we didn't have any major plans to celebrate, I longed to be home with him and our young son. There were no more scheduled events as part of the launch festivities, no direction other than to just sit tight. So, I decided for myself that there was really no need for me to stick around, and I should just go home to my little family the next morning as originally planned.

About an hour after making this seemingly insignificant decision, I ran into the Vice President of the satellite program (the big man in charge that week at the Cape). As we approached each other in the hallway of the hotel where we were staying, he stopped me and asked something about the logistics of that afternoon... what were we all supposed to do while we waited patiently for the weather to cooperate, allowing him to finally launch his multi-billion-dollar baby into space.

He was a man whose silent, stoic gaze wasn't necessarily mean hearted but was just cold enough to make you nervous whenever you were in his presence. As he spoke, he looked at me and past me at the same time, as if I wasn't worth his actual, full attention. I answered his question about the logistics and then let him know I'd be heading home in the morning as originally scheduled. When I told him this, he finally took a moment to look me directly in the eye and asked why I was going home before the rescheduled launch. He asked, not out of concern for me missing a once-in-a-lifetime chance to see a satellite launch in person, but out of concern for himself and worry over who would continue to run the show behind the scenes.

I knew I was nothing more than a glorified swag-bag-giver-outer and that I really wasn't needed there, especially at that point after all the festivities were over and all there was left to do was wait and watch. The people who *really* needed me at that point were 3,000 miles away. I gave my VP the simple explanation "Oh, it's my husband's birthday tomorrow and I gotta get home to my son. Besides, you don't really need me here!" I kept my voice upbeat and sincere, downplaying my planned absence. I also realized the decision that was a no-brainer to me was apparently unimaginable to him... a man whose entire career was culminating in the moment he was now waiting to happen the next day. He replied with some mumbled acknowledgment and walked away.

The next morning, I got up well before the sun to catch my flight home. I had a feeling of freedom as I drove west to the Orlando airport, my baby waiting for me at home and my boss' baby still waiting on the launch pad behind me. Later that afternoon I arrived home to my eager husband and 19-month-old son. I will never forget the moment that baby boy saw his mom after five days, the longest he'd ever gone without me. He threw his chubby little arms around me and embraced me like best friends after they've gone years without seeing each other. Recently turned 33-year-old Michael also gave me a warm hug, knowing what I had "sacrificed" to be there. In that moment, I knew I had made the right decision to leave behind some superficial career opportunity for the true happiness of my family.

Know Your Priorities

Throughout my career, I've seen countless people who base their actions on what *other people expect them to* value and

prioritize, rather than their own values and priorities. I used
to be one of these people. Whether at work, at home, in my
relationships, in the quiet of my own thoughts, I always said
"yes" to something if it met any of the following three criteria:

1. It's something I find important.
2. It's something I want to do.
3. It's something *other people think **I should** find
   important or **I should** want to do.*

Of course, #3 is the problem that we're here to address
and ultimately eliminate. But first, it's important to notice that
#3 doesn't simply say "something other people find important
or want to do." Other people's priorities are fairly easy to say
"no" to. What it specifically says is things that "other people
think *I should find important* or *I should want* to do." The
pressure isn't just to do what other people value, but it's to
internalize those values and priorities as your own. It's the
things that society expects you to think are important; things
that society expects you to want to do. See the distinction? It's
not enough to just begrudgingly do something that others find
important. It's more complicated than that. We're expected to
actually think it's important, by our own assessment.

Take the example of the satellite launch event. Earlier on
in my career, I would have never left the event early. Had you
asked me if it was important for me to stay, I would have
correctly answered, "No," since I had no significant role to
play. Had you asked me if I wanted to stay, I would have
correctly answered, "No," because I wanted to get home to my
husband and young son. But I would've stayed anyway
because other people like my VP expected me to think it was

important and expected me to want to stay. My VP didn't expect me to stay simply because it was important to him. He *expected me to also think it was*

important. This is why it's so hard to Lean Out of things that fall into that third criteria. You're not just saying "no" to someone else's priorities; you're saying "no" to their expectations of your priorities.

> You're not just saying "no" to someone else's priorities; you're saying "no" to their expectations of your priorities.

"Right-sizing your life" is about eliminating things that fall into this tricky third criteria, but it's far more easily said than done. For one thing, some of us have been doing things that fall into #3 for so long that we've truly internalized them as things we ourselves find important (#1s) or want to do (#2s). These are the things that were ingrained in us all the way back in early childhood.

In my case, Leaning Into my career – or being "successful" in a high-profile corporate job – was my ultimate #3. I had been convinced by the Lean Inners of the world that it was my duty as a modern woman to achieve as much as I possibly could. I had been convinced by my corporate upbringing that pursuing promotions and recognition was something I *should* find important and I *should* want. Again, I didn't Lean In simply because I was told to or because they were important to someone else. I was Leaning In because the world expected me to think it was important to do so.

More recently in my journey, I came to realize that such professional accomplishment was neither important to me nor something I wanted. In reality, it was just a #3. Once I realized this, everything started to make sense.

I finally understood why, after years of pursuing different jobs in different companies, none of the positions ever gave me the sense of fulfillment I had been seeking. Early in my career, I achieved an admirable level of "success" in those roles and I appeared to be someone who was Leaning Into her very promising career. And if that was important to me and something I wanted to do, why didn't I feel the sense of accomplishment and fulfillment that came with the Lean In message? I now realize it was because such achievement was actually not truly important to me or something that I actually wanted.

It is this exact realization that I believe millions of women like us are having or are on the brink of having. As so many of us reach mid-career level, achieving the "success" we thought was important to us and we thought we wanted, we still don't feel fulfilled. But we don't know why. We're doing all the things that the Sheryl Sandbergs of the world have told us we should do, but it's not as gratifying as we expected.

Is taking that Director position something that *you* think is important or *you* want to do? Or is the desire to climb the ladder something that was instilled in you by others, convincing you that you think it's important? If your honest answer is you think it's important or truly want to do it by your own assessment, then great! Go for it! But if you find that your own opinion is no, you don't see the importance and you don't actually want to, then stop pursuing it.

It's crucial to understand that each answer can - and should - be different for all of us. What is a #1 or a #2 for you might not be for your neighbor, your co-worker or even your spouse. Just as we have to understand that everyone chooses their own immortality projects, we also need to respect what other people determine as their #1s or #2s.

If one woman from Group G determines that climbing the corporate ladder—Leaning Into her career—is important and/or she wants to do, we need to respect that. Likewise, if another woman decides that climbing the ladder is *not* important to her and *not* something she wants to do, then that decision should also be respected.

What matters is that you decide for yourself which things fall into categories #1 or #2 and don't do things that fall into your category #3.

> Decide for yourself which things fall into categories #1 or #2 and don't do things that fall into your category #3.

This framework for evaluating opportunities and behaviors in your life works for large decisions but also with the small, daily choices we make. Let's take a very common scenario that most parents can relate to... the upcoming PTA meeting at your child's school. Should you go?

> *Person 1:* There isn't really anything pressing on tonight's agenda, so *I don't think it's important* that I go. However, the parents are all so wonderful and I really enjoy getting out of the house and socializing in the school community. So, *I want to* go. I Will Go Because **I Want** To.

> *Person 2:* I don't really enjoy socializing with the other parents so, *I don't want to* go. However, there is a very important topic being discussed tonight that directly impacts my kids, so *I think it's important* that I go. I Will Go Because **I Think** It's Important.

Person 3: I don't really enjoy socializing with the other parents so, *I don't want to* go. And there isn't really anything pressing on tonight's agenda, so *I don't think it's important* that I go. I Will **Not** Go Because I Don't Want to, and I Don't Think It's Important.

Person 4: I don't really enjoy socializing with the other parents so, *I don't want to* go. And there is nothing pressing on tonight's agenda so *I don't think it's important* that I go. But other people expect me to want to go, or they expect me to think the meeting is important. I Will Go Because **Other People Expect Me to** Want to or to Think It's Important.

It's okay to be Person 1, 2 or 3, but the goal is to not be Person 4.

Just as it's important for the individual to make her own choice, it's also important that we all respect each other's different choices. This is where mom-shaming can creep in, where we basically try to impose our own #1 and #2 onto other people (basically trying to make it a #3 for them). I've found that the root of mom-shaming and this behavior is the individual's own insecurity in her choice about #1 or #2, or more specifically, the things she has decided do NOT meet #1 or #2 for her. This demonstrates Becker's description of human conflict as people with opposing immortality projects trying to minimize that of others in order to make theirs feel worthwhile. We are all adults and we should all be respected as able to make the right decisions for ourselves. And we should all have the confidence to make and adhere to our own priorities, and to not feel peer-pressured to do what others think we should feel is important or want to do.

Also, keep in mind that your answer can vary from instance to instance. Sometimes it will be "yes" and sometimes it will be "no." Even I answer an occasional work email at 11pm at night if it's something I really want to do, or I think it is important.

Now, you might be tempted to still say "yes" to something even if it doesn't meet #1 or #2, simply because you have the bandwidth or extra time to do it (which you will inevitably have once you start saying "no" to a bunch of things). Because we've all been conditioned to judge each other by how busy we seem, you may be afraid to have any open space in your life out of fear that others will see it as laziness or selfishness. But if you determine something is a #3, don't feel obligated to do it simply because you have the extra time. The point of eliminating #3 items from your life is to have open space to breathe, to take care of yourself, to just enjoy the things that matter to you. So please, leave open space open.

As I've perfected the art of saying "no" and leaning out of those #3s, I've ended up with extra space in my life for the first time ever. As a result, I play with my kids more, exercise more, and I've even taken up piano! The point of saying "no" isn't to make room for some other damn obligation. Your list doesn't always have to be full! The point of saying "no" is to end up with space leftover once you do only the things that are your #1s or #2s.

> The point of saying "no" is to end up with space leftover once you do only the things that are your #1s or #2s.

Don't do things just because you're concerned others will judge you if you don't do them. I know, this is a toughie for those of us who are people-pleasers to our core. But if you use the simple criteria of #1 and #2 above, saying "no" actually becomes pretty easy. Just as I did back in 2012 when the satellite launch was delayed. For my VP, staying and waiting for the delayed launch was a solid #1 and #2. But for me, it was a #3, so I was out of there. The same is true for pursuing promotions and roles of increased responsibility and pay, for PTA meetings, for putting on makeup in the morning. *Do I think it's important? Do I want to do it?*

The concept is actually a pretty amazing tool. Ever since I structured this framework in my mind, I can literally see how I use it in all my decision making on a daily - hourly - basis. It works 100% of the time, without fail. From what you do with your 30 minutes of "me time" in the evenings to whether or not you take a new opportunity at work. Try it for yourself and see! You can even grab a piece of paper, jot down a few things that are the most consuming in your life, and think through which are truly a #1, #2, or #3. And stop doing the #3s! Start with the smaller, less life changing things and the clearer you become on your own criteria, the easier it'll be to evaluate the bigger things, like Leaning Into your career.

For fun I thought I'd share some of my #3s with you. Just remember that everyone's criteria are different. If one of my #3s happen to be a #1 or #2 in your life, that's perfectly okay!

#3s I Lean Out of at My Kids' Schools:

- *Class Birthday Treats* - My kids get a birthday party and their classmates don't need more junk food or trinkets. I don't enjoy doing it and my kids don't seem to care, so we don't bother.

- *Chaperoning Field Trips* - These sometimes meet criteria #1 or #2 for me. I try to drive on at least one field trip each school year for each of my kids. But definitely not all of them.

- *Many of the Extra Curriculars* - When our oldest son entered elementary school, I began to dread the seemingly innocent "Friday Folder" that comes home chock-full of volunteer flyers, fundraiser events, and endless extracurricular sign-ups. At first, I was in my old people-pleaser mode and my initial reaction was to say "yes" to *everything*, especially if I technically had the bandwidth to do it. But I quickly realized that surviving the school-age years with three kids was going to be a marathon, not a sprint. I needed to pace myself. So, I started saying "no." And you know what? I survived! My son survived! Actually, we're *thriving* because our lives are full of only things we say "yes" to because they are truly *important*, or we really *want* to do them! Come to think of it, this is another advantage of following this framework.

3s I Lean Out of at Work:

- *Schmoozing During the Lunch Hour – Now that I work from home I'm not as burdened by this social norm. But in my office days, this was a regular battle.* Of course, when it was lunch with the team to celebrate a special occasion, I joined because I wanted to. But otherwise, you would find me eating leftovers at my desk so I could get home sooner to my family.

- *The Late-Night Email Login* - Sometimes there's a crucial email I need to send. But if I were to log into email each night, just out of habit or for the heck of it, I'd end up tending to things that really could wait until the next morning.
- *Happy Hours and Social Events* - The main purpose of these events is typically to "network" and schmooze. Since I'm not trying to climb the ladder, they don't usually benefit me in this way. I am very effective at building relationships with my co-workers and business partners during work hours. And since my immortality project is my family, my after-work-hours usually go to them.

3s I Lean Out of in My Personal Life:

- *Holiday Cards* - This used to meet criteria #1 and #2, but it has become fairly pricy and time-consuming to make the cards, order them, and mail them, all with pictures I already post on Facebook anyway. So, this one no longer makes the cut for me.
- *Friends' MLM Parties* - I love getting together with a group of awesome women to drink some Chardonnay. But I don't enjoy buying candles or stretch pants while we do it. If a particular girlfriend needs some extra support in a new venture of hers, then it might be a #1 and I will support her. Otherwise, it's a #3 and I'm out.
- *Clothes, Hair & Make-up* – I've never been someone who's enjoyed clothes or make-up, so this is a big #3 for me now that I work from home. My hair is usually

in a messy bun and I rotate through endless pairs of
leggings while my old trousers and pencil skirts collect
dust in the closet. Of course, sometimes dressing up
is important, like if I'm having coffee with a potential
client. Sometimes I want to, like when Michael and I go
out to a nice restaurant. But on an average weekday,
you'll find me in leggings and a hoodie.

Keep in mind, in order for this framework to actually
work, you have to be very clear and honest about what "makes
the cut" for #1 and #2 for you. It might take some real soul
searching if you haven't taken a step back and looked inside in
a while. Also, your own criteria can change over time. Maybe
when you were right out of college, Leaning Into your career
was a #1 or #2 but maybe now, at this point in your life, it's a
#3. What you deem to be a #1 in your 30s when your kids are
young and demanding might not be a #1 in your 50s when
those kids are grown and (hopefully!) out of the house. It's
normal for your answers to change through different seasons
of your life. So, it's important that you regularly reassess your
feelings about certain priorities and opportunities. Even the
decision to attend that PTA meeting or not. One month it
might be a #3 and a "no" but maybe next month there's a very
important issue on the agenda so that month it's a #1 and
#2 for you! Again, it all comes down to self-awareness. And
continuing self-awareness as you and your life change.

Gut Check: What have you been saying "yes" to in your life
purely because they are a #3? What would happen if you
started saying "no" to them? What would you be able to do
with that empty space?

Be Willing to Make Changes

In the Fall of 2016, I returned to the software startup after my third maternity leave. Fortunately, after years of riding the carousel of job changes, trying to find something intrinsically fulfilling, and even changing roles within the company, I had finally found a position that I liked as a manager in the Business Operations team. I was leading interesting projects, solving challenging business problems, and working with fun and very bright co-workers, on a team led by Alex who, as demonstrated previously, was herself a mother of young children.

But even though I was finally doing something I enjoyed professionally, I was in survival mode. I had a one-and-a-half-hour commute (each way), a husband who had just become a teacher, so was throwing himself into his career change, and we were raising a four-month-old, a three-year-old and a six-year old. I felt like I was barely making it at work and barely making it at home (barely making it in *life*).

One morning, a co-worker (a fellow working mom) asked me how I was doing with everything. I told her "I feel like I'm performing 80% at work and 80% at home." My co-worker looked at me with shock and admiration and said, "Monica... That's ONE HUNDRED AND SIXTY percent!"

The math was simple. Objectively, I totally understood and agreed with her point: what I was accomplishing in life was absolutely amazing. But the math still didn't bring me any reassurance. I still felt like a failure.

Another milestone in our Pierce family whirlwind that fall was when my oldest son started kindergarten which meant our family would start our grade school years. Along with this came Room Parent sign-ups, class parties, field trips, and new social circles - for my son *and for me*! I met dozens of new, wonderful women, many of whom happened to be stay-at-home parents.

Until then, I had never really known any stay-at-home-moms because I had been working full time since I graduated college. Everyone I interacted with were my family, friends from college, or co-workers (who, if they had kids, were obviously also working parents).

Meeting all of these stay-at-home moms was new territory for me. Joining into their circles, doing the class parties and the field trips and even the moms' nights, I often felt like a fraud. They talked about who had *this* teacher, and what Little Jimmy was doing in *that* class, and what new program was being proposed by the PTA. I knew no one and nothing. I had no relevant contributions to make to the conversations, since most of the topics in *my* life at that time were IPOs, enterprise applications, or high-maintenance SaaS customers.

Around this same time, my experience at the Palo Alto software startup was just as alienating. I was in the office by 8 a.m. (after leaving the house at 6:30 a.m.) and worked my ass off for eight hours straight. No lunch breaks, no water cooler chat, no socializing - I even worked while I was strapped to my Medela in the mothers' room (no more time for personal reading on my Kindle). I had a "hard-stop" at 4:30 p.m. each day so I could hopefully miss most of the traffic and pick my kids up from childcare by 6 p.m. Having such firm boundaries and priorities made me an oddball among my co-workers, most of whom were 20-something singles or 50-something millionaires. Not many of them could relate to my lifestyle or my priorities.

But in a culture where your value is based less on your actual work and more on how well you play the politics game,

I began to feel backlash for not Leaning In by Silicon Valley standards.

Even with a proven record of stellar performance that was highly visible to company leaders, and with managers who claimed to have fought for my advancement in the closed door "calibration meetings," I was questionably bypassed for promotion multiple times. Alex had been asked to leave the company and had been replaced by someone less experienced but more eager. I, too, was being phased out of the valuable role I had once played in the organization and saw my assignments going instead to younger, more "dedicated" employees who appeared more willing to Lean Into their careers because they liked hanging around the office until the late hours of the night.

At that point, I had been Leaning Into my career for over 10 years, doing all the things a young woman with my potential and opportunity was supposed to do in order to achieve professionally. But hurdles like the biased startup culture and unreasonable demands I wasn't interested in meeting, steered me away from the path I had been following my whole career - my whole life.

If I had continued trying to Lean In, it would have been a daily struggle to push aside my true priorities like family and personal time and continue pretending my job was my greatest priority. It was a struggle that just wasn't worth it. I didn't quit climbing the ladder because something was blocking me or because of some inequality. I stopped climbing because I just didn't want to be any higher on that particular ladder. When it was 5 p.m., I just wanted to go home to my family. When my child was sick, I just wanted to stay home and hold her. I was fortunate to have a job where I technically was able to do so. But I didn't scramble to answer emails in between her cries, keeping up the façade that I was Leaning In. I was too tired to log back on to my computer at night and opted instead to relax on the couch with my husband and then just head to bed. I wasn't Leaning In anymore, and I didn't care.

All the while, that 80% + 80% = 160% statement continued to linger in the back of my mind. If I was living 160% of an 'average' person's life, why did I feel so inadequate in all areas of my life? Then it finally occurred to me to think about those respective 80%'s *in isolation*.

When I was at work, I was only about 80% of the "standard" employee as judged by the number of hours in the office and/or online. The other employees were reaching 100% of those expectations. Their work was their immortality project and their greatest priority. Amongst the more entry-level employees, they were all roommates, best friends, and a number of them even got married to each other. They worked around the clock and lived and breathed our company – a perfectly fine choice for them, since it's what they'd chosen for themselves. But for someone like me who had priorities outside of my work, I was viewed as subpar, like something was wrong with me.

Similarly, when I was with the other moms from my son's school, I was only able to be about 80% of the "standard" mom. The other moms were giving 100% of themselves to their role as parents. They knew everything and were everywhere when it came to their kids and school involvement. They didn't have to accommodate work meetings or make other arrangements for their kids when something came up at the office.

> As an individual, I was performing at 160%. But at any given moment, wherever I was, I was reaching only 80% of the standard for that particular role.

As an individual, I was performing at 160%. But at any given moment, wherever I was, I was reaching only 80% of the standard for that particular role.

As much as I truly enjoyed the work I was doing at the software startup, I was tired of pretending like my career was my greatest priority. Leadership at the startup didn't seem to like this unusual set of priorities I had, and it quickly became clear to me that it was time for me to find another job – hopefully one that would cut down on my three-hours-a-day commute, allow me to apply my skills in a valuable way, and respect that I was a human being with priorities other than my career.

Ultimately, I found a new job just 10 minutes from home, with a company that values employees based on their performance rather than an unhealthy commitment to their job, where I'm viewed as giving 100% even though I don't go to the happy hours or pull all-nighters sleeping on the couch in the office lounge. I no longer received the same reactions when telling people where I worked as I had at Lockheed Martin or the software startup, but I didn't care. The external approval no longer mattered. I just wanted to be able to do my job and go home at a decent hour to be with my family.

On the mom front, I reminded myself that just because I might not know who's who at the PTA meeting and I might not drive on every single field trip, that didn't mean I was less of a mom. My 80% is damn good. It doesn't matter what the other moms are giving.

It took a lot of personal reflection to arrive at this place where I've now accepted that my 80% is good enough. I will never be a full-time mom and I'll never be an employee whose job is her first priority. And I don't *want* to be either of those things. I love having my first priority being my job as a mom and I also love working full-time. But that means it is physically impossible for me to measure myself against full-time parents or employees who put their job first. So, I stopped. And I don't. I'm just the best working parent I can be.

That change I made from the Silicon Valley startup to the local, slower-paced company was crucial to enabling me to live the life I wanted to be living. Sometimes the changes we need to make are small, like stepping down from a volunteer position that was more of a #3 than a #1 or a #2. Sometimes they are bigger, like finding a job with a different company. Sometimes, if we need to go a completely new direction in our life, we make life-changing decisions, like ending a marriage or moving.

If through your process of self-reflection, you realize certain parts of your life are not aligned to your true #1s and #2s, have the courage to make changes in your life. Sometimes it takes getting creative and being extra resourceful. But the first step is being willing. The challenge is to truly believe in your heart that it's okay to live the life *you want*. Yes, others might judge you: seeing what great potential you have as a professional and viewing it as a "waste" that you've chosen a lower-profile job, chosen to reserve your mental and physical energy for higher priorities like your family. And you might be faced with constant reminders of the opportunities you chose not to pursue. But hold firm to your convictions and be confident that you have chosen the right life for yourself. Surround

> Hold firm to your convictions and be confident that you have chosen the right life for yourself.

yourself with people, companies, and media that respect your priorities and support the type of life you've chosen.

Gut Check: What changes could you make to right-size your life? From turning off LinkedIn notifications to hanging around like-minded friends to moving out of state, what are some easy and small to very large and life-changing things you might do?

Be Honest with Yourself and Others

When I was interviewing for the new position with the local, slower-paced company, I found myself sitting in an impressive boardroom talking with the CIO. We were having a very engaging conversation about the role of enterprise applications in a modern organization and my own interests and experience in managing projects and processes around such technology. We also chatted about less formal topics like the beauty of living and working in Santa Cruz, California, and the contrast from its bustling neighbor, Silicon Valley, from where I was hoping to escape.

Towards the end of our conversation, he pulled out one of the classics from Interviewing 101: "So tell me... where do you see yourself in five years?"

I could have answered with the obvious response we all know we're supposed to give, the one that affirms our singular focus on career progression and nothing else. It's an answer I'd been reciting in interviews for years and almost slipped out without me even thinking about it. "Oh, I'd like to become a Director and then eventually I want to be CIO, just like you!" with a cheery smile on my face. But I did think about it. I had been identifying my #1s and #2s in my life and had realized that raising my children was my immortality project, and I did not want to climb the corporate ladder. So, instead of giving the safe answer we've all had drilled into our heads by career counselors, I decided to answer honestly.

"Well, my family comes first. So, while I want to have a career that is challenging and rewarding, I also want a career that allows me to raise my family and spend time with them. So, I can't tell you where I necessarily want to be in five years, because as opportunities present themselves, I will make career decisions based on what is best for me and my family." I went on to talk about the type of work I knew I wanted to do and how the role I was interviewing for was a great fit for me.

After the interview, I reflected on the answers I had given, feeling great about some, second-guessing myself on others. This particular one had been a risk. I couldn't quite tell if it had sealed the deal or lost me the job. I had a feeling it had sealed the deal as I'm a pretty good read of people, and the CIO seemed in the moment to have appreciated my response. But I didn't know for sure until the job offer came in a few days later.

It was a minor moment in the grand scheme of things, but it represented a mindset change for me. Instead of pretending to be a career woman who wants to go as far as she possibly can up the corporate ladder no matter what the price, I was honest with myself and with someone else about who I really am.

I wanted to do the job, to be challenged and use my skills to help advance the company, to earn a paycheck, and then go home to my family. It was a respectable truth and I realized that if I were honest about it, people would still respect me, as a professional and as a person. Anyone who didn't respect me or couldn't understand my choice wasn't someone whose approval I needed anyway.

It takes guts to be honest. I took a chance when I decided to be honest with my CIO. He could've decided to not give me the job because I "lacked ambition" by the standard corporate definition. But even if we work up the courage to be honest with ourselves about who we truly are, even if we decide we want to Lean Out, it doesn't do much good if we're still too afraid to be honest with others about that choice - if we still "fake it 'til we make it" or give the clichéd interview answer, "I want to climb the ladder!"

> Even if we decide we want to Lean Out, it doesn't do much good if we're still too afraid to be honest with others about that choice.

In addition to being good for ourselves individually, such honesty can have a positive impact on the thousands of others who are in a similar position. If more of us start speaking up honestly about our priorities and our choices, the corporate culture and society in general might start to acknowledge our perspective and realize we don't all have to be Leaning Into be valuable.

For example, lately I've noticed many women claiming to have found a way to "have it all" through a trend in work-from-home jobs such as virtual assistants and multi-level-marketing. I often see them posting on social media about how this job has allowed them to finally "have it all"! I appreciate their sentiment and the fact that they've chosen to follow their own path, but I would encourage them to stop doing so under the guise of "having it all." You can't claim to have finally achieved something if you did so by changing the definition. The fact remains that, instead of having a high-profile professional career (which is part of society's definition of "having it all"), these women are opting instead for more modest work that is either more fulfilling to them or allows them the flexibility to live the way they want. Again, an outstanding choice they've made that I, too, have basically made. The point is, this is a great opportunity for these women to say "Hey, I've decided I just don't want to 'have it all' and that's okay."

It might seem petty or like insignificant semantics to argue over what we call this choice these women have made, but it's actually a very valuable opportunity to show others that these women have stood up for what they actually want, declined the socially acceptable path, and instead have made a different choice that's right for them. Because society makes it so taboo to admit we don't want "it all," people are afraid to say it this way and instead finagle the definition to make their choices more acceptable by society's standards. If they really want to inspire others and effect change, then I encourage them to just admit they chose not to "have it all" and that that's okay!

Gut Check: Have you been honest with yourself and with others about who you truly are and what truly matters to you? If not, what is holding you back from doing so? What would happen if you started to be more honest?

Set Boundaries and Find Allies

A few months ago, I decided to try out a tactic I'd seen other co-workers use but hadn't yet used myself. Since in our corporate world everything is dictated by people's Outlook calendars, and since my family responsibilities are my greatest priority in my life right now, I decided to add a block to my calendar to show me as unavailable until 8 a.m. every day, since I have to take the kids to school each morning. I figured I might as well add one at 4:30 p.m. each day when I need to leave to pick my youngest up from daycare by 5 p.m., followed by that evening's Family Time which is my greatest priority.

The purpose of the blocks is to show me as "unavailable," which would reflect my online "status" as such if anyone were looking for me at these times. It would also discourage co-workers from scheduling meetings with me during those hours. But of course, I make exceptions when it's actually necessary for my job. And as a project manager, I'm usually the one scheduling all the meetings I have to attend anyway. So really, the blocks were there to serve me more than anyone else, as a very tangible representation of my priorities and my boundaries.

But after a few weeks of this new calendar approach, my director noticed and confronted me about it. She asked how I would accommodate early morning meetings and I reassured her that, of course, I would make other arrangements if a pressing meeting had to be held during off-hours. Then my director's attention shifted from my ability to accommodate schedule conflicts that I knew would be infrequent, and she began to challenge whether or not I was working "enough hours," an awkward accusation since my performance and accountability had been nothing but stellar since working for her.

Her issue appeared to be the fact that I was literally defining my workday to be eight and a half hours each day. Apparently, something was wrong with that. I again attempted to reassure her that, when I start work in the morning, I go hard all the way until I have to wrap it up for the day. I'm not chatting at the water cooler or participating in other office distractions. I like to think that my 40 hours is equivalent to the average employee's 60 hours in terms of productivity. In response to this, she then claimed she was "concerned about me," that I should take a break in the middle of the day so I could recharge. I thought to myself, "Lady, I have three kids, a full-time job, a household to run. 'Recharge' is not in my vocabulary. You expect me to sit and eat my sandwich and do nothing for 30 minutes? I haven't 'done nothing' since 2009." What she seemed to be telling me was I needed to be less efficient so that it took me longer to get my work done.

She finally pulled out all the stops and got to the root of what must have been bothering her. She said, "If you just don't have enough work to do, we can give you more. You know, most people don't have the luxury of working just 40 hours a week."

First, I was appalled that she thought I didn't have enough work to do. Even though I had had nothing but excellent performance since joining her team a year earlier, my skill and value were being questioned just because I'm able to do my job more efficiently than most people, or because I wasn't willing to play corporate politics and inflate the amount of time I spend working just for appearances' sake. Second, I thought, how horrible a management style she had that measures someone's performance based on how many hours they're sitting in front of their computer. How exhausting to have to constantly keep tabs on your direct reports by reviewing their calendars and checking their Skype status. Third, I thought about how appalling it is that this is the general perspective in the corporate world: the opinion that it's nowhere near good enough to get into the office at 8am, put in an honest day's work, then leave eight hours later to go home to your family. As my director put it, that's a "luxury" that we shouldn't expect to have.

I had been working under this director for over a year and decided I couldn't work under her leadership style any longer. As much as I liked the work–and was good at it–it wasn't worth constantly stressing about whether or not I "appeared" to be working enough hours. I had a very honest conversation about it with my director's boss, the CIO I had interviewed with over a year earlier. Because of the honesty I had had with him from the first day we met in that interview, he knew who I was and what mattered to me. He knew I was a reliable, well-performing employee who happened to put her family before her job. And he respected that. He confirmed that I added great value to our team even though I worked "just" 40 hours a week. With his reassurance, I continued in the job and soon found myself under new leadership. To this day, I'm still working in the same job, still 40 hours a week, and a little more when the work requires it!

In this story, a few things happened that were crucial to the end result. First, over a year earlier, I had been honest with my CIO about who I was. This enabled me to be myself without having to feel guilty or second-guess how I would be received. Second, because I had set that precedent, I was able to set boundaries for myself. In this case, that meant only working 40 or so hours a week and putting tangible indicators in place like the Outlook blocks, to enable me to live aligned to my personal priorities. The problem, in this case, was that the understanding I had with my CIO did not seem to trickle down to my director. She didn't seem to understand or support my values; that my family was more important than my job and that I wasn't willing to work more than 40 hours a week when the work didn't require it. Fortunately, I had my CIO to back me up. And that is the third piece of the puzzle that fell into place. I had an ally. Someone who knew the real me and was there to defend me and enable me to continue to live the life I've chosen for myself. In this case, I was willing to leave my job and find a different one that would better respect those priorities (back to the earlier point of being willing to make changes). But the ally relationship with my CIO was strong enough to outweigh the conflict with my director and I didn't have to leave.

In addition to finding allies who support the choices you've made, it's also helpful to eliminate things that might challenge those choices or cause you to second-guess yourself. One of the best examples of this that I've encountered is our use of social media. On an app like Facebook, we are presented with filtered versions of our friends' and families' lives. We see only what they want the world to see... the most impressive, most beautiful 1% of their otherwise average, maybe even ugly lives. Just as Facebook presents us with these filtered versions of our personal lives, LinkedIn does so with our professional lives.

Of course, the way these apps increase user engagement is through notifications. LinkedIn is no exception. Having a fairly large network on LinkedIn, I used to receive a few dozen notifications each day. Whenever I'd see that a former colleague had been promoted to VP of some up-and-coming startup, or a former classmate from my MBA program had been elected to a coveted position in our local government, it would remind me of the professional life and opportunity I had chosen to walk away from. The pit in my stomach wasn't a result of lacking confidence or a figurative glass ceiling that the others had somehow managed to crack. Their accomplishments, while wonderful for them, served as constant reminders of the opportunities I had chosen to decline. They were like manifestations of my old self, still taunting me with what I "should be" doing.

So, to protect myself and my choices, I turned off my LinkedIn notifications. I rarely use it now, only to learn about some new contact or client. But I go out of my way to not try and keep up with what Joe is doing or what Sarah has accomplished, not because I'm not happy for them in their pursuit of their immortality project, but because I don't need to constantly second-guess my own choice.

Gut Check: Are you evaluating your true priorities and being honest with yourself and others about what they are? Are you willing to make changes to better align your life to those priorities? Do you set boundaries and find allies to help you protect those priorities?

Although it often feels like it, we are not beholden to a society that demands certain choices from us. We don't have to accept the corporate environment as it is and squeeze ourselves uncomfortably into it. But the alternative – "right sizing" our lives and living the way we choose – requires action and confidence on our part. We have to be ready and willing to challenge the status quo by speaking up about another option, and actively choosing what we want rather than passively taking what we're given.

Chapter 5 *With Our Partners*

> "The thing that I'm most proud of and the thing
> that brings me the most happiness, is my family."
> *- Mark Zuckerberg*

When I started my new job at the local, slower-paced company, I was delighted to find myself surrounded by other professionals who also seemed to value their balance and openly spoke of priorities they had outside of work. It was a refreshing departure from the startup culture I had left behind, where the expectation was that the company and your job were your life.

Of course, there were still some exceptions, like my director who didn't understand my need to work "just" 40 hours a week. There was also one particular co-worker who stood out from the balanced, slower-paced crowd. Rohit was the definition of Leaning In, willing to do whatever it took to get the job done, always looking for opportunities to do even more for his team and the company. He was the type of guy who thrives in the corporate world and is usually referred to as a "top performer" because he gets all of his work done, and then some. Rohit played the corporate game, attending and often organizing all the company events and team extracurriculars. He was the guy sitting in the very front row at the all-hands meetings and chatting with executives in the hallway. Rohit's dedication was great for the company and his team members but, upon further inspection, it was horrible for him.

As I got to know Rohit as a person, I learned that he was struggling. As the father of two young children and husband to a woman who had a very high-pressure, high-demand job, he often spoke about wanting to be there for his kids more, wanting to devote more time and energy to his marriage. He also mentioned his disappointment with the fact that he'd been neglecting personal priorities such as exercise and hobbies.

We often label people like Rohit as "workaholics." The people who usually earn this label have made their career their immortality project so, as their greatest priority, they put it above everything else in their life, or they have other immortality projects but they've become addicted to external validation (as the term "workaholic" implies). In Rohit's case, I had enough insight into his personal life to know that his career was not his immortality project, but that he had come to rely on the external approval he got from being "that guy," the one everyone knew walking down the halls, the one everyone wanted on their team because he always goes above and beyond. He was dependent on that label of "top performer" and was willing to do anything to keep it, even if he didn't know why, and even if it meant his personal life suffered because of it.

Around the time I met Rohit I was also beginning to write about Leaning Out. As I was developing the concept, I was especially interested in observing it and I couldn't help but notice that this colleague–now friend–of mine was the quintessential Lean Inner who might secretly want to be a Lean Outter. But, considering the Lean Out concept is most relevant for modern professional *women*, the most interesting takeaway from my observations of Rohit was the fact that he was a man.

Men Can Lean Out Too

Did you know Elon Musk has five kids? Or that Mark Zuckerberg, one of the most famous CEOs in the entire world, has been quoted as saying "The thing that I'm most proud of and the thing that brings me the most happiness, is my family"? Probably not. Because their role as a father isn't what we know them for and not what history will remember them for. Based on modern society's values of money and power, men might feel they are more likely to "be remembered" and leave their mark on the world through their professional achievements rather than the impact they can have as fathers.

Fortunately, this mindset is shifting among Gen X, Xennial, and Millennial fathers, who are arguably the most loving, involved fathers of modern history. I believe this evolution of their paternal role is due largely to more equality in the male-female domestic relationship, where the woman can now work in an equivalent profession making comparable money to the man and the man, in turn, can contribute more to household duties and family responsibilities than he has traditionally done. Even though he's not famous for being a good dad, the fact that Zuckerberg publicly made such a statement about the personal importance of his role as a father, speaks volumes about this evolution in our social roles.

But this transition for our male partners has not been without its own set of challenges. While modern working mothers struggle with the pressure to have a professional career while still raising children and maintaining their home, we often overlook the stress felt by modern working *fathers* who are pressured to pursue traditional careers and now also be more involved at home and in raising their children. They've been asked to become equal partners at home and are encouraged now more than ever to be involved in the lives of their children. But while we've enabled men to Lean Into their roles as husbands and fathers, we still expect them to make their career their immortality project. As a result, they are expected to achieve the same level of professional success they've always been expected to pursue as the "providers," *plus* support their partner with home responsibilities and make time to have involved relationships with their children.

Because of social norms and perhaps some biological reasons, men are more likely to choose their career over the raising of their children as their immortality project, or at least feel *pressured* to make their career their immortality project, like Rohit. As a side note, I believe this is why men are more inclined to "play the game" and climb the ladder in the corporate world: because they're more likely than women to make their career their immortality project which makes them more willing to bend over backwards for their career – work the 60 hour weeks just for visibility, go to the happy hours and schmooze with the VPs.

But as more modern men feel the desire to prioritize their role as fathers over their role as professionals, the Lean

Out challenge is just as real for them as it is for us women. The challenge for a father who works in the corporate world but whose greatest priority is his family, is that he, too, is faced with the issues described in chapter three, all the ways corporate culture hinders their ability to have any priority other than their job. Like modern professional women, men too feel obligated to pursue professional "greatness" since that is the only way to receive external approval from society and from within the corporate world we work. The main difference between the pressure men and women feel is men are not obligated to Lean In in order to demonstrate the equal opportunity their gender has only recently obtained. Men feel obligated to Lean In because society tells them they are valued for being providers.

The take-away for us is that our men might feel similar pressure to Lean Into their job while secretly wanting to make parenthood or any other passion in their life their immortality project, rather than their career. Being true to ourselves and Leaning Out is not only important for us but for enabling our male colleagues and our partners who struggle with the same issues.

Your Greatest Ally

Just as it's crucial to have allies at work like co-workers and leaders who understand and support your personal priorities, it's just as important to have allies in your personal life like family and friends who support your choices and will enable you to live the life you choose. If you have a spouse or life partner, this person is in the unique position to be your greatest ally.

It's important to reiterate that Leaning In or Out of one's career isn't about one choice being right and the other wrong.

It is about recognizing that either are valid choices and all individuals deserve respect and support in whichever choice they make. Plus, there are infinite levels of distribution you might choose between Work and Life. However, finding the balance that's right for you becomes more complicated when you are in a committed partnership like a marriage. You might find yourself in a partnership where you and your partner have made similar life choices (like Michael and I who both split ourselves pretty evenly between Work and Life, as represented by Scenario D in Image 4). Alternatively, you might be in a partnership where one of you chooses to prioritize your career and the other decides to prioritize something else. Based on

Scenario A. *Traditional Roles*

	Work	Life	
Women	0%	100%	100%
Men	100%	0%	100%
	100%	100%	

Scenario B. *Corporate World Expectations*

	Work	Life	
Women	100%	0%	100%
Men	100%	0%	100%
	200%	0%	

Scenario C. *What Typically Happens*

	Work	Life	
Women	75%	40%	115%
Men	75%	40%	115%
	150%	80%	

Scenario D. *A Leaning Out Couple*

	Work	Life	
Women	50%	50%	100%
Men	50%	50%	100%
	100%	100%	

Image 4 – Leaning Out Together

Becker's observation that the root of all human conflict arises from individuals trying to convince others that their choice of immortality project is more worthwhile one than someone else's, these opposing choices can be challenging in a marriage. These opposing choices can be the source of arguments if one spouse dedicates his or herself to work while the other dedicates his or herself more to their family or home life, and both feel undervalued or underappreciated.

But if two partners who have chosen different immortality projects can respect each other's choice and make the logistics of their daily life together work under such a scenario, it is very possible for them to support each other and be happy in their respective roles. The extreme version of this is in the Traditional Roles depicted in Scenario A, where women typically devoted themselves to Home life, men to Work life, and if both parties were happy about their respective commitments, everyone was satisfied with the arrangement.

The challenge comes when both partners are working professionals, in a corporate environment that is built on the assumption that every employee is Leaning Into their careers, committing themselves 100% to their Work (as depicted in Scenario B). The corporate world's assumption is that "someone else" is handling all childcare, housework, and all personal demands that employee might have in their life (represented by the 0%s in Scenario B). But in reality, as individual employees each with their own job, both partners are pressured to fully dedicate themselves to their respective employer and that leaves no one to care for the Home side of the partnership.

As a result, the Life responsibilities must be picked up by both, in addition to their supposedly full dedication to their Work. In order to preserve just enough time and energy for their Life, working parents fall short of the expectations of corporate America (represented by their respective 75%'s in Scenario C). They can't stay late at the office or go to the happy hours but often attempt to make up for this seeming lack of commitment by doing the late-night emails.

Because both individuals are trying to Lean Into their careers by meeting unrealistic expectations set by the corporate world, while simultaneously working with their partner to fully cover their Life responsibilities between the two of them, both individuals end up overstretched (represented by the 115% in scenario C). To make things worse, if one individual is actually wanting to Lean Into his or her career, he or she is unable to because they can only muster up that 75%. If one individual wants to dedicate him or herself to their Life (like the raising of the kids), they feel like they're falling short (represented by the 40%'s in Scenario C). In such cases, the individuals are unable to devote the attention they'd like to their immortality projects and end up feeling resentment towards their partner for not being able to support their pursuit of their immortality project.

Furthermore, the Life side of this couple's situation is falling short (represented by the combined 80% in Scenario C) because they are both so overstretched, they're unable to commit as much as they'd like to the Life side of their partnership. This can manifest itself as parents who aren't as engaged as they want to be with their children, a household that becomes messy and stressful, no time for exercise or family dinners, postponed vacations, or deprioritized personal hobbies. All of this because both members of the partnership are trying to Lean Into their corporate jobs.

In order to get from Scenario C to Scenario D—to reach a state of balance as individuals and in the life you share together—you must be honest with yourself and with your partner. Talk with each other about what you both individually want – *actually* want, not what society expects you to want. Then come up with an arrangement that supports each of you. If one person truly wants to Lean Into their career, then perhaps the other is okay Leaning Out to tend to more of the Home commitments. Or, if both truly want to Lean In, the pair agrees to some Life changes to accommodate that. Whatever the resulting arrangement is, make sure it's born out of an effort to give both members an opportunity to pursue their own immortality project, to strike their own desired balance between Work and Life. Ideally, your two respective preferences will complement each other. If they don't, both members will have to make some sacrifices. But as long as you are both honest with yourselves and each other, you can hopefully find an arrangement that works.

> Whatever the resulting arrangement is, make sure it's born out of an effort to give both members an opportunity to pursue their own immortality project.

In my and Michael's case, we have a situation close to Scenario D. We both have professional careers but we both want to commit a good amount of ourselves to our Home life. As a result, neither of us have impressive, high-powered jobs, but we have balance within ourselves and within our family, allowing us to enjoy our children and the life we've built together.

Gut Check: How can you enlist your partner to be a great ally for you in your effort to "right-size" your life? How can you and your partner work together to find a balance that enables both of you to pursue your own respective immortality projects?

In 2019, there was a quote that went viral on social media, having originated from journalist Amy Westervelt's book *Forget 'Having It All': How America Messed Up Motherhood - and How to Fix It.* Westervelt says, "We expect women to work like they don't have children and raise children as if they don't work" (Westervelt, 2018). I would expand this to say the same is true for men. The corporate world expects women and men to work like we don't have children. The inhuman expectation on men is just as big a part of the problem. Just like my friend Rohit, many men want to put their families first, too.

Additionally, I would round this quote out to say, "It's time parents start working like we have children!" And this is precisely what I mean by Leaning Out. It doesn't mean completely quitting our jobs or slacking off as employees. We simply need to "work like we have children," or any other priorities in our lives, for that matter.

Chapter 6 *For Each Other*

"It is not in numbers, but in unity, that our great strength lies."

— Thomas Paine

Extend the Women's Movement

The original women's movement wasn't about getting more of us into the boardroom (as Sheryl Sandberg tried to convince me as I sat pumping in the mothers' room in 2013). The movement was—and always has been—about our freedom: freedom to have a professional career, freedom to not have a professional career, freedom to raise children, freedom to not raise children. We've become so obsessed with all the things we can do – having it all, doing it all –that we've forgotten that the choice to not do them is just as important. The overbearing message of the modern women's movement has ironically cannibalized (or at least stigmatized) our original role as engaged partners and mothers.

In this regard, the concept of Leaning Out is not *counter* to the women's movement, rather it's an *extension* of it. Leaning Out is about giving us back the original rights and privileges that we lost sight of while we were so focused on gaining new ones. Most women who fought for our gender to have the opportunity to achieve great professional success didn't intend for that opportunity to come at the cost of being able to be engaged, loving partners and mothers. Yet, generally speaking, that's where those of us in Group B and beyond now find ourselves.

We've become so focused on getting the freedom we were missing (professional opportunity), that we lost sight of our original values (family, personal balance) and have inadvertently alienated those who simply want the original option.

Just as we should have the right to pursue a high-powered, high-demand career, so, too, should we have the right to choose *not* to. Leaning Out doesn't necessarily mean quitting your job entirely and becoming a stay-at-home-parent (although this choice is also a perfectly respectable one). Yet this is often how people initially interpret the Lean Out message. It speaks volumes that this is the automatic response and demonstrates how binary our society views a woman's role: you're either a highly ambitious professional or you're 'just' a mother. If you choose not to be the former, it's automatically assumed you are choosing to be the latter.

But as we addressed in chapter three in regard to Balance, there is a whole spectrum of lives we can lead between these two extremes. The level of investment we choose to place in our careers and in our personal lives can consist of any number of combinations. True, 50 years ago we weren't allowed to have careers, so that variable was always zero, leaving the other 100% to be focused on our roles as mothers and wives. But now, with professional opportunity, it doesn't mean we have to invest that 100% entirely into our careers. It doesn't mean we all now have to strive to be CEOs. It doesn't have to be all or nothing. Leaning Out doesn't mean you have to quit your job and go home, and having a career doesn't mean you have to strive for the top at all costs.

Still, we were raised with this expectation that we will achieve as much as we possibly can professionally. And it's a really hard expectation to shake. The reason it's so hard to shake is because it's more than just an independent demand from our parents to do as we're told. The expectation is actually more complex than that. We're expected to have *internalized* this ambition. The pressure is not just to achieve, but to want to achieve. The pervasive message is that all women of our generation are supposed to want to be the first female president or the first CEO of their company. In our culture where more is always better - more money, more power, more hours worked, we're supposed to innately want the greatest professional success we could possibly reach. No one ever mentions that it's okay if we rather maintain a mediocre career that allows us the flexibility to have the life that we want.

Now, as our entire generation begins to reach the peak of our professional lives, our children reaching the demanding school-age years just as our aging parents begin to require more care, and as our energy is depleted and our mental and emotional health is plummeting, we're realizing that we've been lying to ourselves about truly wanting all this professional success which, unfortunately in our modern world, comes with 24/7 demands and pressure. Or maybe we did sincerely want it at one point (probably before we had kids and other aspirations for our lives). And now perhaps we've started noticing our professional ambitions waning. But we tell ourselves this is due to a lack of confidence, a fear of failure, sexist leaders, logistical challenges, or any other common scapegoat for why women don't achieve "greatness" in today's world.

But our waning ambition is not due to any of these reasons. The real reason we don't achieve all that we're capable of is that the higher we climb and the more we look around at what it means to "have it all," the more we're saying, "thanks, but no thanks." The more we understand what this equal opportunity means (while still wanting to be engaged parents, have fulfilling marriages and have a life outside our careers), we're realizing maybe we got more than we bargained for when we started pursuing it back in the '60s.

> The cliché question of whether or not it's possible to "have it all" is irrelevant. The real question is, do we even *want* to "have it all"?

The cliché question of whether or not it's possible to "have it all" is irrelevant. The real question is, do we even *want* to "have it all"? Millions of us are starting to question the attractiveness of the "have it all" scenario. We understand and can appreciate the argument that women as a whole need greater representation. We need to continue fighting for those still stuck in Group A. And who wants to be the one to let down their entire gender? No one wants to be the one to speak up and say, "You know, thanks for all this equal opportunity and everything and, I guess I could be CEO, but I'll pass." So instead, we make up explanations for these doubts we secretly have about our professional ambition and continue the pursuit to "have it all" with our heads down.

The primary reason I wanted to write this book was to speak up for the hundreds of thousands of women (and men) who have no desire to Lean Into our promising corporate careers yet remain silent because it is socially taboo to admit such a thing. I want us to treat our desire for recognition as an extension of the women's movement. Instead of the one-sidedness of the mainstream message which wants to see all women Leaning In and achieving as much as possible, let's follow the message up with, "but it's also fine if you don't have ambition to run the world."

Just as we have to stand up to sexual harassment, gender bias, and unequal pay, we have to stand up to narrow-minded corporate assumptions that pigeonhole us into a singular definition of what it means to be a valuable professional. The choice to work a hard 40-hour week but go home to our families, to not have "ambition to run the world"... these choices also need to be on the list of things we're fighting for.

> We have to stand up to narrow-minded corporate assumptions that pigeonhole us into a singular definition of what it means to be a valuable professional.

We need to challenge managers who tell us we need to work more hours, not because our performance or the work requires it but simply because it's the norm in the corporate world. Just as I was prepared to quit working for my 'Lean In' director who told me I don't have the "luxury" of working "just" 40 hours a week, we need to get comfortable standing up for our priorities and our personal boundaries. Of course, we don't always "just quit" a job, but the general point is to stop blindly accepting the standard for what is required in order to be a valuable employee. It shouldn't matter where you work, when you work, or even for how many hours you work – as long as you're getting your job done.

Contrary to Sandberg's argument that we need more women in formal, high-ranking positions to effect change for the rest of us, I say you don't have to be a VP or above to make a change. There are hundreds of thousands of us—managers, senior managers and directors—educated and professional women living and working in the middle ranks of the corporate world, and we are *already* in a position to affect change. As a workforce of women, we don't need to push a few elite individuals to the top especially if those individuals, like Marissa Mayer, aren't going to affect change anyway. Instead, we need to band together and speak up right from where we're standing.

> There are hundreds of thousands of us—managers, senior managers and directors—educated and professional women living and working in the middle ranks of the corporate world, and we are *already* in a position to affect change.

In July 2019, when I was knee deep in the development of this book, a friend brought to my attention a new book she had just seen called *Lean Out: The Truth about Women, Power, and the Workplace,* by Marissa Orr. My initial reaction was utter devastation over the fact that another author had seemingly beat me to the market with the same book. But once I got my hands on a copy and dove in, I realized that the Leaning Out concept is not a singular idea that one person has. It's a mindset. It's a movement. Not only did I realize there is plenty to be said to warrant my own book, but I felt thankful to have Ms. Orr's voice adding to the strength and validity of the Lean Out message.

The more of us speak up about who we really are and what is really important to average working women in the corporate world, the more people will stop pushing us to fit the Lean In mold. The more honest we are with ourselves and with others, the more we can live the life we truly want rather than the one we feel obligated to live.

Sharing such a message will take time and patience. One book (or even two) will not change the corporate world or mainstream perspectives overnight. But it's a start. Voices like mine, Orr's, and hopefully yours will eventually be heard as we continue to speak up.

Enable Others

Since I began sharing my Lean Out perspective, the most frequent response I've received from readers has been one of relief in knowing they are not the only ones who have this perspective, and gratitude for my willingness to speak up and share it.

Of course, it's very encouraging to know that my words are impacting others and helping you find the permission to live your authentic lives. But these expressions of thanks are bittersweet. It's unfortunate that so many of us feel like we can't speak up about how we truly feel and who we truly are, that when just one woman does so, it's viewed as some significant feat. Which is why I want us to think about this as a movement. The conversation has started, but we have to make sure it continues. There are millions of women out there, like me and you, who secretly feel like they're the only ones who lack the professional ambition that every other modern woman seems to have. The more we all start to be honest about who we truly are, what we truly want for ourselves, our careers, our families, our lives, *and* we speak up about it and are honest with others, then the more empowered other women will feel to do the same.

Just like my call for honesty from those who are declining to "have it all", instead of force-fitting your version of it into the mainstream definition, simply state that you're declining to "have it all" in favor of having "just what you want." The more

> The more of us speak honestly about our values and our choices, the easier it will become for other women who feel the same way.

of us speak honestly about our values and our choices, the easier it will become for other women who feel the same way, and we will eliminate the stigma associated with the choice to "just" be average.

Gut Check: What are some ways you can help voice the alternative perspective of Leaning Out?

Leading Those Who Lean Out

Much like my CIO who defended my value and my need to work a "luxurious" 40 hour workweek or the VP from the startup who took a sabbatical at the peak of his career to spend time with his teenage kids, we need leaders who recognize that their employees are human.

Instead of reprimanding us for having an immortality project other than our career, we need to seek out leaders who recognize that we can still be valuable employees. As long as we do our job, it shouldn't matter if we have other priorities.

If a leader you work for is attempting to push you to adhere to ineffective expectations of the corporate world, like working more hours just for the sake of visibility, challenge that old-fashioned way of thinking. Enlist one of your allies to support you in your effort to hold true to your own choices and your boundaries. Be prepared to make changes as extreme as finding a new company to work for if your current one can't accommodate your life choices.

Companies and leaders who don't understand this will find themselves missing out on a pool of quality talent, as we take our skills to companies and leaders who do understand and respect us.

> Companies and leaders who don't understand this will find themselves missing out on a pool of quality talent.

In addition to supporting the individual choices of their employees, leaders also have the important responsibility of setting the standard for what is expected of the rest of us. They therefore have the power and influence to change those expectations. This is why it's especially important for those in leadership positions to actually take that vacation, to not send or respond to emails after hours, and to periodically leave work at 4pm to go to their child's soccer game.

We don't need another book, another women's leadership conference, a law mandating maternity leave, or another COO telling us to Lean In and do more, giving us "tips" for how to stretch ourselves even thinner. If we really want to enable women in the workplace, we need women and men who are respected, accomplished professionals to demonstrate that it's okay to be actual humans.

We need more leaders to Lean *Out* as a way of giving permission to the rest of us to actually use that work-life balance the recruiting brochures like to brag so much about. We need to know that we will still be considered for that promotion even if we only work an average of 45 hours a week and that we don't have to sacrifice our families and other personal priorities just to prove how hardworking we are.

For those of us who aren't in positions of leadership, we can encourage such behaviors from our leaders. When you see someone in a position of influence make such a decision - a director not responding to email for a week because he's on vacation or a manager declining a promotion because her children are young and she wants to be able to continue to prioritize them... make sure to thank that leader for their example. Let them know that you don't respect them any less for Leaning Out. If you're like me, you actually respect them a whole lot more.

Gut Check: If you hold a leadership position managing others, do you have reasonable expectations of them? Do you equally value those who have priorities outside of their job, so long as they get their work done? Do you set an example by being honest about and respecting your own priorities outside of work?

If Lean In advocates really want to affect change and broaden professional opportunity to more women, rather than urging women to do more, more, more in order to reach positions of power within the confines of modern standards, I think they would have a greater impact if they applied their influence towards changing the standards. Success in the corporate world shouldn't require 60-hour workweeks or cutting your maternity leave short. Putting work before your family as a way of proving your commitment to your career shouldn't be the standard. Simplify the entrance criteria. Lower the bar – or *humanize* the bar - so that it's actually feasible for today's working women to succeed.

Final Thoughts

I had spent all morning on November 22, 2017, running around the house cleaning and preparing to host about 20 family members for Thanksgiving the next day. The folding tables and chairs were set up, the tables draped with forest green tablecloths and autumn-themed centerpieces. The hand towels in the bathrooms were carefully folded and the serving platters were lined up on the island, ready to be stocked with Michael's amazing roast turkey and all of our family's favorite side dishes.

While I thoroughly enjoyed hosting such gatherings, it was a lot of work and I always put unneeded pressure on myself to make it "perfect." I also realized later that aside from about three cups of coffee, I had skipped breakfast that morning and in all my running around, probably hadn't drunk as much water as I usually do.

That afternoon, after enough cleaning and preparation had been done, I wanted to reward my seven-year-old son for having quietly entertained himself all morning, with a little outing for just the two of us. As we drove through town headed towards Henry Cowell State Park with plans to take a leisurely stroll through the peaceful redwoods, I started to feel like I couldn't breathe.

Of course, this sudden sensation itself made me panic even more. My heart rate began to quicken, and I felt as if my body was going into a type of "fight or flight" mode, but from what perceived danger, I had no idea. Out of habit, I quickly called my mom to tell her what was happening, like telling her would somehow make it stop. But it didn't. It just got worse. My heart was racing, and my breath felt farther and farther away from me. With my first-born helplessly strapped in his car seat in the third row and me behind the wheel of our two-ton SUV, I panicked even more at the uncertainty of what might happen next.

In the middle of a two-lane road through the redwood mountains with no cross streets for another mile or two, I found a wide enough spot on the side of the road to pull off. Of course, my son wanted to know what was going on and since there was a very real chance he might be about to witness his mother passing out, I told him as much as I could, as calmly as I could, and gave him the best instructions I could think of. "Stay in your seat, don't leave the car. Here's my cell phone in case..." *Oh wait, should I call 911 before something happens to me?* I was alone with my seven-year-old on the side of an isolated road and afraid I might pass out at any moment, so I decided to call. Once I could accurately describe where I was, the dispatcher sent a response team to me.

Just as I was really feeling stupid for having called 911, the paramedics fire truck pulled up. As I embarrassingly climbed out of my car and walked over to the paramedics, one kind firefighter checked on my son, and they had a nice chat about Pierce fire trucks.

The paramedics talked me through the situation and checked all my vitals. They patiently listened as I explained the day I'd had and the physical issues I'd experienced. They assured me it was good I had called, better safe than sorry. But just when I thought I had pulled myself back together, my mom drove up. She had tracked me down after my phone call had left her feeling this was more serious than I was letting on. Like any grown woman who has been holding it together for 35 years, seeing my mama come to my rescue, I lost it all over again.

Eventually, the paramedics drove my car to a safe location in a nearby neighborhood and my son and I rode back across town with my mom. In the coming weeks, I continued to have panic episodes, mainly when I was driving. I would feel a rush of lightheadedness and then a racing heart every time I got behind the wheel. The counselor I had been seeing told me how revisiting the scene where such an experience happened can trigger it to happen again. I was very fortunate to have the support system I had, who helped with kid drop-offs and pick-ups and even getting me rides to work.

These seemingly-out-of-nowhere panic attacks prompted me to investigate what was stirring so violently in my soul. I consulted with doctors, counselors, self-help books and my inner circle, trying to identify the cause of this very real, physical anxiety. The answers I got were along the lines of, "you're doing too much" and, "even happy stress is still stress." But none of these explanations seemed right.

At that point in my life, I had become fully aware of my priorities and had spent the prior year or so "detoxing" from external approval. I had started saying no to all the #3s, and I'd realized that Leaning Into my career was actually a major #3. I had found a less prestigious but more flexible job that was closer to home and one I could do with my eyes closed, just the right amount of challenge but no extra stress or pressure to climb the ladder. My marriage was solid, and our kids were happy and healthy. For the first time in my life I was not stressed and was truly happy with the life I was living.

So why now? Why did I begin having anxiety at a point where I was arguably the most balanced and the most at peace? It occurred to me that it was the process of accepting that new-found balance and right-sized life that was triggering these emotions. It was the fact that, for once in my life I didn't have any stress, and it was a foreign, uncomfortable feeling. My anxiety was actually the Lean Inner in me refusing to go down without a fight. It was my 20-year-old people-pleasing self rebelling against this older, wiser self who had finally admitted that the external approval she'd been pursuing really wasn't important.

> My anxiety was actually the Lean Inner in me refusing to go down without a fight.

Earlier in the book I described my addiction to external approval and how my introduction to intrinsic fulfillment through motherhood finally kicked that addiction. Well, these anxiety attacks were my "withdrawals" from the old external approval that my body had literally come to physically crave. As I subconsciously came to terms with the fact that I was foregoing all of the professional accomplishment and recognition I had been pursuing my whole life, I was struggling with what that meant for my future.

Even though I had begun to live my life in the way I truly wanted, I was now confronted with the fact that I was giving up any possible future achievement and external approval. I was deliberately and out loud saying no to being some impressive business professional with a high-level title and a corner office. I would never be a keynote speaker at a "Women in Business" conference. I would never have that hit of external approval when telling people about my impressive job title at my famous employer.

I was also acknowledging the error of my prior ways, by letting go of the deeply entrenched desire to please others. I began to revisit and second-guess every decision I'd made thus far, every turn I'd made along my path. *Wait, why hadn't I pursued my passion for Architecture even though it supposedly wouldn't yield as many job prospects as a career in Business?*

Not to mention the guilt. What about all the women (and men) who fought so hard so that I could even have the chance to climb the ladder? What about all the women out there who, according to Sheryl Sandberg, were counting on me to have ambition to run the world? Was I letting them all down by admitting that I didn't want to be someone amazing and impressive? That I was okay just being average? Was I an anti-feminist because I decided that my greatest priority in life was and would always be my marriage and my family?

In addition to embracing my new, balanced Leaning Out life, I also had to say goodbye to my old life, my old mindset. And it wasn't easy to do. For 30-some-odd years I was hyper-focused on success and accomplishment. It wasn't easy to just give all that up, even once I knew that the alternative was a much better fit with who I truly was. I had to go through a period of mourning the person I thought I was. I had to accept that I was Leaning Out and let the guilt and uncertainty wash over me for a time. For me, that rush of emotion, that process of letting go of who I used to be, came in the form of panic attacks.

With this onset of anxiety, distancing myself from triggers became critical to my happiness, even crucial to my health. Even though at that time we lived on the outskirts of Silicon Valley, I was still surrounded by people who'd chosen their careers as their immortality project. The countless Teslas whizzing by, the obvious CEOs in their "casual Friday" jeans talking into their earbud while waiting in line at Starbucks. They were all constant reminders of the corporate ladder climbing I was trying to permanently release from my life. They were constant reminders that, by society's standards, I was no longer pursuing the "right path" and would never be considered "successful." It made managing my anxiety and my ability to Lean Out of my career much harder.

So, when Michael and I started discussing the idea of moving out of California, even though we had nonchalantly discussed the idea multiple times over the past 12 years, this time we were both a bit more serious about it. Just three months after randomly mentioning the idea, we up and sold what we thought was our "forever home" in California, bought a new home in Idaho, coordinated my transfer to become a remote employee continuing my job with my employer, found Michael a new teaching job in Idaho, and enrolled the kids in new schools.

Much like my journey to Leaning Out, our move was unexpected but just felt right. It was a very literal change as we left behind neighbors who were billionaire venture capitalists and Stanford MBAs, and now had neighbors who were farmers and small shop owners. But it was a figurative change, too. It represented my saying "thanks, but no thanks" to the opportunities I had grown up with in Silicon Valley. It meant admitting that I didn't need or even want the things

I thought I had wanted, like the corporate title or owning a million-dollar California property. It meant instead thinking about what type of environment I actually enjoyed being in, realizing why I always had an urge to get as far away from the office as I could when leaving work each day.

For me, when I closed my eyes and dreamt of the life I wanted, I didn't see myself sitting in a leather chair in a corner office overlooking a view of the city. I saw weekend adventures in the outdoors with my kids and quiet weekday nights snuggling with Michael on the couch. I dreamt of financial freedom and the flexibility to pursue professional dreams I never would be able to pursue while I was strapped to a California mortgage. I saw a quiet town in a community that didn't care about the valuation of your startup, but instead about the values you were instilling in your children.

Sitting in the passenger seat as Michael drove us across state lines, the kids in the back surrounded by boxes of possessions that were too valuable to throw on the moving truck, I was literally leaving behind my #3 life.

Even after moving to Idaho, my decision to Lean Out—and my ability to find peace with that decision—is regularly challenged by the fact that I still work every day in corporate America. Even though I've decided to Lean Out, I'm continuously tempted with offers of external approval and pressures to make my career my immortality project. Leaning Out in a world that wants you to Lean In is not easy. But if you really want to live the life you choose and not the one you feel obligated to live, it is possible. At a very high level, here's what it takes:

- Be very clear on your #1s and #2 and Lean Out of your #3s

- Be honest with yourself and with others about what's actually important to you
- Be prepared to make changes to better align your life to your priorities
- Set boundaries and find allies who will help you live the life you choose to live
- Be prepared to let go of your former self and what "could have been"

Let It Go

If you have a *Frozen* fan in your house, then you probably know all the words to the Disney movie's infamous anthem, "Let it Go." And if you're like me, it's secretly one of your favorite songs.

One morning last December, after I had finished the daily school drop-off routine, I headed back home to "the office," cozy in my personal work attire of leggings and a hoodie, when the season's first dusting of snow began to fall. During the five-minute drive home, I could see it quickly accumulating in the fields and farmlands that lined our Idaho suburbia.

It was just a few months after our unexpected, life-altering move to Idaho and for this California girl, it was the first time I had ever seen snow where I actually lived. It was fresh. It was new. I paused to think about our new life and what it meant for me and the path I could now follow. I had Leaned Out of the career path I was on in Silicon Valley, the life I thought I wanted to pursue back in the Bay Area. For the first time in my 35 years, I felt like I was where I was because I had *chosen* to be there. I was doing the things I was doing because I had *chosen* to do them.

Maybe it was the fresh snowflakes or the rush of freedom and relief, but I felt a sudden urge to blast my secret favorite song (the single version by Demi Lavato, of course). With my car windows down and snowflakes hitting the left arm of my hoodie, on the heels of a major move and amidst a career change from corporate stooge to freelance writer, in a new place and living a new life as the new me, I belted the words like I was Queen Elsa herself. I'd left behind a life of obligation and was now discovering a new version of myself that had been aching to get out all along.

In Elsa's case, she was tired of concealing who she truly was and decided to Lean Out of the version of herself that she felt obligated to be. This is what it's like to stop climbing the corporate ladder, take a look around, realize you don't want to climb any more, and in some cases even get off that ladder entirely.

Yes, you might lose the external approval you once were so dependent on when you were Leaning Into your corporate career. No, you'll never be honored publicly for choosing to prioritize your role as a mother. You'll never be on a Forbes' *Top 30 Under 30* list for being a balanced human being. Yes, you might feel guilt or uncertainty for leaving behind the person you thought you should be, who you know you could've been, but you'll be too relieved to grieve.

If you turn out to be nothing more than a great mom, a loving wife, a good person, and a reliable middle manager with an average career, I think you've done pretty damn good. The rest of it? Let it Go.

Works Cited

Becker, Ernest. *The Denial of Death.* New York, Free Press, May 8, 1997.

Brokaw, Tom. *The Greatest Generation.* New York, Random House, May 1, 2001.

Crosby, Tripp. "A Conference Call in Real Life." *Tripp and Tyler,* January 22, 2014, https://www.youtube.com/watch?v=DYu_bGbZiiQ.

Hollis, Rachel. *Girl, Stop Apologizing: A Shame-free Plan for Embracing and Achieving Your Goals.* HarperCollins Leadership, March 5, 2019.

Jebb, A.T., Tay, L., Diener, E. *et al.* Happiness, income satiation and turning points around the world. *Nat Hum Behaviour.* 2, 33–38 (2018) doi:10.1038/s41562-017-0277-0.

Milo, Daniel S. *Good Enough: The Tolerance for Mediocrity in Nature and Society*: Cambridge, Harvard University Press, June 18, 2019.

Orr, Marissa. *Lean Out: The Truth about Women, Power, and the Workplace.* HarperCollins Leadership, June 11, 2019.

Rath, Tom. *StrengthsFinder 2.0.* New York, Gallup Press, February 1, 2007.

Sandberg, Sheryl. *Lean In: Women, Work, and the Will to Lead.* New York, Knoph, March 12, 2013.

Sincero, Jen. *You Are a Badass: How to Stop Doubting Your Greatness and Start Living an Awesome Life.* Philadelphia, Running Press, April 23, 2013.

Westervelt, Amy. *Forget 'Having It All': How America Messed Up Motherhood—and How to Fix It.* New York, Seal Press, November 13, 2018.

Acknowledgments

As a first-time author, getting this book in front of the eyes and ears of readers was a very long and often discouraging process. But I never felt alone.

To my friends and followers on social media, including the women who allowed me to share their experiences within this book, and Heather Borah whose "Lean Out" bracelet gave me the inspiration to see this project through, thank you for continuing to share your stories of Leaning Out. This book exists for and because of all of you.

To those I met at Mount Hermon Christian Writers Conference: you were my first exposure to the world of writing, and you lit a fire inside my soul. And to the friends and mentors I've met through Idaho Writers and Editors Association, including Donna Cook and Troy Lambert, thank you for giving so freely of your time and energy.

To Laura Yorke and the other literary agents and acquisitions editors who said my writing and message had potential, thank you for your encouragement.

To the many women I've worked with over the years who've shown me what it means to be a valuable and respectable professional while also being a woman, a mom, a human being; you are the women we should be honoring and writing books about. You are the women I look up to. And to the exceptional leaders I've worked for - men and women - who practice balance in your own lives and also show humanity toward your employees, please continue setting this important example.

Thank you to the team of professionals who helped take my idea and make it into an actual book, including my editors, Cristen Iris and Gill Hill, for providing invaluable feedback, Sara Cox and Jake Kuwana from Kampfire Media for creating compelling marketing materials, Dane Low and eBook Launch for their beautiful cover designs, Rob Price at Gatekeeper Press for holding my hand through the publishing process, Diane Lasek and ListenUp Audiobooks for helping me get my message to audiobook listeners.

To my friends and family including Sierra, Kate, Sarah, Michelle, Bridget, Lynn, Elizabeth, Kathy, and Grandma, who continued to humor me when I went on and on about this "book thing": thank you for your endless encouragement.

To my parents, Diane and Tom, for demonstrating what balance and true happiness looks like and for always supporting me and allowing me to find my own way, even when it meant moving your grandchildren out of state. Thank you for all you've given me.

Last but most importantly, to my husband, Michael. You love and support me whether I'm leaning in, leaning out, upside down or sideways. There's no one else I would rather be with on this journey.

CPSIA information can be obtained
at www.ICGtesting.com
Printed in the USA
BVHW032309221120
593949BV00011B/94/J

9 781642 378786